Flashes in the Fog

PRAISE FOR FLASHES IN THE FOG

This is a *must read* for those who are grieving... This book should be in every church library and grieving ministry! – M. Williams

I loved this book! The author takes you on her personal journey of surviving a very difficult situation. Its a book that shows you that God is concerned about every aspect of our lives, no matter how small or large. This book is very inspiring and witty at times. I highly recommend this book! – Amazon Reader

Very comforting for someone who has lost a loved one... I have ordered several of these books to give to friends in mourning. – V. Smith

I was uplifted and carried on a journey to a new awakening in my spirit. This is a must have to assist with the grieving process. This book will at times take you back and move you forward but always leaves you with hope. I brought several and passed them on to others that have lost and they have all said *"Thank you! This was just what I needed*!" – P. Banks

A *must read* for everyone going through a grieving process and for everyone who knows someone going through it. It should be a part of every church's grief ministry's library. There is so much that needs to be known by family, friends and church members. A great source of information. I wish that I could afford to purchase this book for everyone I know! – Amazon Reader

OTHER TITLES BY ARLENER STEELS-POYDRAS

Danielle in the Lion's Den:
A Devotional for Women in the Workplace

Available at:
Amazon.com
Barnes & Noble (bn.com)
Apple iBookstore

Arlener Steels-Poydras

Flashes in the Fog

How God Spoke to Me in the Midst of Unexpected Tragedy, Crippling Grief, and Sobering Disappointment

Flashes in the Fog

Copyright © 2017 by Arlener Steels-Poydras

Printed in the United States of America

All rights reserved. No part of this publication may be used or reproduced, stored in a retrieval system or transmitted in any way by any means, electronic, mechanical, photocopy, recording or otherwise without the prior permission of the author except as provided by USA copyright law.

For permissions, please address correspondence to:
Arlener Steels-Poydras, P.O. Box 181376, Arlington, TX 76096.
www.artis-the-artist.com

Second Edition

Print ISBN: 978-0-9985026-2-5
Ebook ISBN: 978-0-9985026-3-2

Cover design by Arjay Garcia

Scripture quotations marked (NLT) are taken from the Holy Bible, New Living Translation, copyright ©1996, 2004, 2007, 2013, 2015 by Tyndale House Foundation. Used by permission of Tyndale House Publishers, Inc., Carol Stream, Illinois 60188. All rights reserved.

Scripture quotations marked (NIV) are taken from the Holy Bible, New International Version®, NIV®. Copyright © 1973, 1978, 1984, 2011 by Biblica, Inc.™ Used by permission of Zondervan. All rights reserved worldwide. www.zondervan.com The "NIV" and "New International Version" are trademarks registered in the United States Patent and Trademark Office by Biblica, Inc.™

Scripture quotations marked (The Message) are taken from THE MESSAGE, copyright © 1993, 1994, 1995, 1996, 2000, 2001, 2002 by Eugene H. Peterson. Used by permission of NavPress. All rights reserved. Represented by Tyndale House Publishers, Inc.

DEDICATION

In memory of our beloved son,
Artis James (A.J.) Prestidge
March 16, 1988 – February 20, 2012
Artis-the-artist.com

An Ode to A.J.

Nine months of feeling you grow inside of me
Nine hours of labor as I delivered my child-to-be
But this labor was one of amazing love
Because I knew that God sent you from above
On February 20, 2012, the sun rose without you
And in my anguish, I truly did not know what to do
The labor pains started again, but this time in reverse
A million times more intense, they felt like a deadly curse
The pain of childbirth is soothed by expectancy
This pain means I must give you back, reluctantly
Again I can't breathe, but Lamaze is no help for me
My soul screams for the future that you will never see
But the reverse labor is something I must go through
It's my way of mentally and physically releasing you
It's been many months now and the pain is subsiding
Only because Jesus has been daily providing
A peace that a non-Christian can never understand
I simply know that you are "still in God's hands"
So "My A.J." get you some good rest
Just like the baby that laid upon my breast
You said in your own words and certainly without a doubt
"I am grateful, and I know God will work things out."
See you in the morning.
Love eternally, Momma

We don't yet see things clearly. We're squinting in a fog, peering through a mist. But it won't be long before the weather clears and the sun shines bright!

– 1 Corinthians 13:12 (The Message)

WEATHER CONDITIONS

	Foreword	ix
	Introduction: The Climate Has Changed	1
1	The Storm Has Arrived	25
2	Zero Visibility (I Can't See!)	29
3	Storm Chasing	51
4	A Perfect Forecast	83
5	This Little Light of Mine	113

FOREWORD

It is an inevitable fact of life that we will all encounter storms – momentary inconveniences that throw us off kilter, disrupt our routines and distract us from accomplishing the things on our extensive to-do lists according to schedule. These are the types of situations that merely annoy us, mentally frustrate us and cause us a degree of emotional discomfort as we seek a solution to resolve them. Though they may cost us time, money and even a little peace of mind, once they are resolved, they are soon forgotten. However, there are storms, and then there are STORMS: massive, ominous disruptions of life that bring us to our knees, devastating us to the core of our very being, and changing our lives forever. These storms are more than momentary inconveniences; they are the ones that drive us to endless tears with a deep ache that cannot be articulated. They leave us feeling isolated, hurt, and many times, alone. These are the storms that we never forget, as their name and the year that they arrived become inscribed upon our very soul.

The difference between a storm and a STORM is like the difference between a rush hour downpour and a category 5 hurricane: one represents an inconvenient, bothersome, yet temporary disruption of our life's routines while the other can represent the utter destruction and devastation of life as we know it, threatening our very survival and ability to go on.

In *Flashes in the Fog*, Arlener Steels-Poydras poignantly addresses the category 5 storm experience that began with the unexpected loss of her 23 year-old son – a parent's worst nightmare. In a matter of moments, what was once the happy, productive and spiritually-focused life she once knew became one in which she was barely able to function. She refers to this season after the storm as "living in the fog." In the fog, things were dark, hazy and lonely. There was no sun, no happiness, no interest, no energy, and no indication of what she should do or where she should go; that is, until God clearly revealed Himself to her in the middle of the darkness through strategically-timed *Flashes in the Fog*!

By allowing Steels-Poydras to see *Flashes in the Fog*, God showed her that He had not forsaken her; He was still there, right in the middle of one of the darkest, most devastating storms that any human can ever experience. Through reading the insightful accounts of the things that God said to her and did for her amidst the storm that He allowed in her life, Steels-Poydras helps us to develop hope in the midst of our own storms and the fog that follows. Her transparent testimonials help us to see that although it may look and feel like we have been deserted by God, He is indeed there with us, giving us hope by showing us flashes of Himself at just the right times – times when we desperately need to know that He is there the most.

Having suffered the loss of my own child, I can personally testify that *Flashes in the Fog* will help anyone who has suffered recent tragedy or who desires to help someone else through a tragedy. Readers will experience the real-life sorrow of Steels-Poydras' storm as if they were right there with her and then witness her transformation in the midst of the storm as God taught her to turn the tables on it. Instead of being a casualty of the storm, she became a *storm chaser* and utilized her tragedy to bring glory to God!

Allow Steels-Poydras' significant work to comfort you through your own tragedy. Learn from her insights and use them to help others navigate their way through the darkness. Utilize her recommendations of Do's and Don'ts to help you minister *the right way* to those who are walking through the dark fog following a storm. Most of all, utilize her work to help you grow in your own faith to believe that when you are going through life's most challenging situations, God's promise is true: He will never leave you nor forsake you. Through it all, although you can't see Him in the darkness, He's right there at your side.

Jennifer Travis Cox
Broken Dolls Non Profit Corporation
Founder/President

INTRODUCTION
THE CLIMATE HAS CHANGED

**When the Unexpected Happens:
Waking Up in the Fog**

Some of the things that you encounter in life will change you for the rest of your life. Sometimes the forecast will announce a storm ahead of time, but other times, a storm can seem to come out of nowhere – a violent disturbance that blindsides you, suddenly emerging on the horizon and showing no regard for the damage it will cause. When these unexpected storms show up unannounced, they often leave a trail of devastation in their wake that makes the destruction they have caused seem irreparable. Without notice, you are left to pick up the pieces after a life disturbance that you never saw coming. As you stand there silently staring at the clutter that once comprised your well put-together life, you find it impossible to even process what to do next. All of a sudden, after the storm, you're in a fog.

When the unexpected happens, especially when it is accompanied by the blinding pain of a tragedy, the mind responds in an unusual way. Despite your best efforts to go on thinking and operating with the same level of conscious awareness and clarity that you are accustomed to in your everyday life, you cannot simply move on. Instead, your mind catapults you into a different type of mental state: one that is hazy and surrounded by a fog that clouds your mind to the point that you recognize that something is noticeably different. Something is *off*. *Yes*, you can still think. *Yes*, you are still aware of your surroundings. *Yes*, you can still reason well. However, it's *different*. It takes so much more effort now to perform the same functions that you could effortlessly perform before without a second thought. In the midst of this fog, you find yourself on auto-pilot, going through life with robot-like motions and performing daily activities and responsibilities without much thought or awareness.

Any unexpected experience associated with any type of loss in life can lead to a season of walking through this type of fog. Such devastating experiences can take on many different forms, including divorce, sickness, the betrayal of a significant friendship, the loss of a job, legal problems, financial ruin, character assassination or even the death of a loved one. Regardless of the type, each of these unexpected experiences comes with an immeasurable pain of its own that is very real, very personal and very tangible to the person who experiences it. No one can adequately compare his own pain to that of someone else's by saying "You think that *your* situation is painful? Look at *mine*! Now *this* is *real* pain!" Therefore, be careful not to compare or discount another person's storm experience with regard to your own, because real pain is real pain, regardless of what causes it or who experiences it. Our emotional responses and reactions to these situations are just as individual as the situations themselves, and so are our scars.

Charting God's Goodness:
Journaling His Track Record

In 2001, as part of my quiet time, I developed the discipline of writing down prayer requests, key events and concerns in the lives of my family members. I also included the outcome of the issues, how God had answered the prayers, whether He had placed me on hold, and even my thoughts during the waiting process. I would then use my journal as a source of encouragement for myself and my family in difficult times. My journals would remind me that I had been in difficult situations before and that God was always there to carry me through them. They were a reminder that I have had some very happy times and God was there, being happy right along with me. Conversely, I have had some bad times, but God was still there to comfort me through them.

What my journal entries supported was something that I knew then and that I continue to know now: God is illimitable, untraceable, omniscient and omnipresent. As great as He is as the Ruler of the universe, journaling was my way of reminding myself, in my humanness, that God is also involved in the smallest details of my life; He is personally and intimately concerned about me. I had no idea that this discipline of writing down the details of my life would be used to identify God's hand in the midst of the biggest challenge that I have ever experienced.

A Story with Purpose:
God is in the Simplest, Smallest Details of Life!

This book is not an attempt to bring an Almighty God

down to my level, to trace His every move or even to put Him into a box; I know that doing so would be impossible! Instead, the purpose of this little book is to show you that God's loving presence is right there in your everyday, mundane activities – even when you are in the midst of a storm of *hurricane proportions*! Our only hope during times of storm like these is Jesus Christ.

Biblical hope is defined as an expectation to receive something that God has promised. Faith is an absolute confidence in God that He will do what He said He would do, an unwavering belief that whatever God has spoken will surely come to pass. Although you've never seen or experienced it yet, you know that what He said He would do is as good as done! Therefore, faith is the substance of our hope, and our hope is built upon the promise of what God said He would do. After reading this book, it is my prayer that your faith will increase to the point that no matter what you are going through, you will never stop believing that God's promise will come to pass. In times of storm, I pray that you would put your faith into action and look for God in the simplest ways and the most unusual of places, because He *is* there!

Flashes in the Fog: Providing Hope in Darkness

The Message Bible assures us in 1 Corinthians 13:12 of the following: *"We don't yet see things clearly. We're squinting in a fog, peering through a mist. But it won't be long before the weather clears and the sun shines bright! We'll see it all then, see it all as clearly as God sees us, knowing Him directly just as He knows us!"* During my storm, there were *Flashes in the Fog*: incandescent flashes of light amidst the darkest fog that were sent by God to provide the hope that I needed to move forward each day. In the midst of your own unexpected time of devastation, He will do the same for you. Oftentimes, you will not understand the significance of the light until its flash has already faded back into the darkness. However, when you are blessed to see these flashes, they will change your life forever, giving you a sense of hope and peace that surpasses all human understanding. In the midst of it all, continue to look for the *Flashes in the Fog*, and know that God will guide you gently through and safely to the other side of calamity where the Son still shines.

1
THE STORM HAS ARRIVED

February 20, 2012: The Call that Started the Storm

In the world of meteorology, there are people who are paid to watch the weather conditions and alert us of upcoming storms that may impact our lives. These warnings allow us to take shelter, make safety preparations and brace ourselves for the storm's arrival. However, occasionally, there are unexpected storms that form suddenly and without warning, with the worst of them leaving behind unfathomable destruction as evidence of the encounter. Such are the storms that go down as vivid memories in our mental database – the ones that we can refer to by name and date, even decades after they occurred, because of their level of remarkable devastation. I remember the exact date of my storm: February 20, 2012.

It was President's Day – a holiday and a day off from work for me. I had planned to do some writing on a long-overdue project. My husband had already left for school, so I snuggled into my favorite housedress and got settled into my office at about 9 a.m. At 9:20 a.m., my cell phone rang. By the time I made it to the phone, the call was missed. I immediately dialed the number back, and a police officer answered. He asked me what my relationship was to Artis Prestidge.

"He is my son," I replied. "Why?" I immediately thought A.J. was in trouble or that he had been stopped for unpaid traffic tickets. The officer then asked me if I was alone, and I said, "Yes." My heart rate began to accelerate.

"I am very sorry to inform you that Artis is no longer with us," the officer calmly said.

"What do you mean by that?" I asked with an elevated voice as my heart continued to race.

"He is deceased," said the officer. Thus arrived the unexpected storm in my life, blasting through with hurricane force.

I managed to dial my husband's cell phone number and screamed some words to him. He was about 25 minutes away, and I guess I screamed for that long, because upon his arrival, I was still screaming; however, no sound was coming out of my throat by that time. I don't remember much about the remainder of that day because a dark fog had settled in over my life.

Taking a Look Back:
Trying to Trace the Weather Pattern

Just like any other storm that suddenly arises without warning, this storm did its damage and then disappeared as quickly as it came, leaving me to pick up the pieces. I tried to filter through a thousand questions that flooded my mind. *How could this have happened? What could have caused this storm? What did I miss? Is there anything I could have done?* As I lay awake later that night, I reflected on the previous day's events, desperately searching for some explanation. Somehow, I thought that an explanation might make me feel better.

I remember that the day before was a typical Sunday evening, and I was texting back and forth with my son, A.J., as we did almost daily. We would watch the same TV shows while texting, talking about our yoga classes and everything else under the sun. Our last communication was Sunday, February 19th at 7:48 p.m. As I was relaxing, a text came in:

A.J.: "Hey, how are you?"

Me: "Fine. You?"

A.J.: "Blessed."

Me: "Good."

A.J. was never much for words!

At 2:15 a.m. on February 20th, a Monday morning, I suddenly awoke with an awful stomachache. I did not want to disturb my sleeping husband, so instead of tossing and turning, I got out of bed, went into the living room and turned on the TV, trying to recall what I might have eaten to cause such pain.

As I flipped through the channels, I picked up my cell phone to see if I had any missed calls. There were none. I thought to myself with a giggle, *I'll text A.J. He's probably up!* We would often text each other at odd hours just to say "Hi," or "Caught you sleeping!"

I changed my mind about texting A.J. because although Monday was a holiday for me, I knew that he would have to get up for work that morning. Instead, I watched TV for a little while and then read my *Women of Faith Devotional* for February 20th. The subject of the devotional for that day was "WWJD?" (What Would Jesus Do?) Looking back at the book, I had highlighted in yellow at 3:45 a.m.: *"He will remind us of the truths from scripture we have stored in our hearts. He will point us to Himself. And in Jesus' name we will be enabled to shed light where there is darkness."* I eventually went back to bed around 4:45 a.m., only to get the devastating news at 9:20 that morning.

There is an unexplainable connection between a mother and her child that can only be given by God. No one had to tell me the time of my son A.J.'s death; I had *felt* it. More importantly, God had given me instructions at 3:45 a.m. on how to handle it. These instructions would prove essential during my storm.

*The storm is only a surprise to us;
it's not a surprise to God!*

Defining Devastation:
My Storm Is <u>Not</u> Bigger Than Your Storm!

As I started the toughest journey of my life, I quickly learned that suffering is the great equalizer. I encountered many people in the early weeks after my son's death whose intent was to comfort me, so they would tell me about the storms they were currently going through or something that had happened to them in the past. Many told of their own losses, ranging from financial ruin, divorce, sickness and even the death of a loved one.

Initially, I felt insulted when a person would say to me, "I know how you feel," or "I remember when I went through my divorce," or "I remember years ago when my family member died." These were all very loving and sincere people who simply did not know what to say. If only they had known that silence was just fine.

The irony of it was that God quickly revealed to me that the pain felt by these people in their individual storms, although different from my own, was just as real, and in some cases, more devastating to them than my son's death was to me. I realized that God wanted to use me to bind up the brokenhearted, even in my own broken state.

Some of the stories that people shared with me were intense and heartbreaking. I was touched by each of them, and my eyes were open to the suffering of other people in a way like never before. Through this, I realized that my storm was not bigger or more important to God, just different. The following are just a sampling of the storm stories that were shared with me (names have been changed for the sake of anonymity).

After 23 years with the same company, Mike was handed a pink slip and laid off from his job. It was the longest relationship he had ever known. He had been married for 15 years with two sons. Mike was *devastated*.

At 35 years old, Gail finally decided to "get healthy" and lose weight. After several months, she had lost 20 pounds and was feeling great. She made an appointment with her family doctor for a physical, which she had not done for years, including a mammogram. There was a spot on the mammogram that turned out to be breast cancer. She had a husband and a 10 year-old daughter. Gail was *devastated*.

High school sweethearts, Carolyn and her husband had been married for 25 years. She was never given any reason not to trust her husband. Arriving home from work early one day, she discovered that her husband had been having an affair with another woman for some time and actually had a two year-old son with her. Carolyn was *devastated*.

Cynthia and Joy had been best friends since elementary school; the two were inseparable. Cynthia discovered that Joy believed negative and hurtful information communicated to her by another person without first asking Cynthia if it was true. Cynthia was *devastated*.

Karl graduated from high school in 2010 and signed up for the military. He was killed in Afghanistan in December 2011. Karl's family was *devastated*.

Devastation is the common thread in each of these

stories. Using a "Hurt Scale" from 1 to 10 (with 10 being the highest level of hurt), can you measure the feelings of the people involved in each situation? I don't think you can. Can you determine which of their storms was more painful? Of course not.

We must realize that we are all fearfully and wonderfully made by God to be different and unique; thus, different people hurt in different ways at different levels for different reasons. For some people, everything hurts like a 10 on the Hurt Scale. When storms arrive in their lives, they are the most devastating and debilitating experiences that they can imagine... to *them*. The situations are absolutely overwhelming... to *them*. You see, we cannot feel what another person is feeling because we are not that person! As much as they can try to describe their pain to us, though we may be able to relate at *some* level, feeling *exactly* what they are feeling at the depth they are feeling it is impossible. The hurt that one person feels with the loss of a job can be just as debilitating as the hurt another person feels at the death of a loved one.

Another ironic thing happened during the season of my storm: with the unexpected death of my son came "unexpected people" with their own "unexpected storms," and they were asking "devastated me" for advice! My initial response was (and I quote), "Is anyone dead?" In retrospect, I realize that I was saying, "My storm is bigger than your storm." However, now I can see that this was the wrong response! It was a selfish answer birthed out of my own pain.

God knows my love for people, especially those who are hurting. Thus, God's way of correcting my response was to continue to send hurting people my way, even in the midst of my own storm, until I got it right. As they shared their stories, I clearly saw that the pain and hurt from their storms was very real – just as real as mine. The source of their pain was different from mine, but I realized that they were hurting just as badly as I was. Hurt is hurt, is hurt, regardless of the cause. My storm is *not* bigger than your storm!

Responses to storms are as individual as the number of people on the earth!

Finding Relief from the Storm:
Breathing, Being & Bowing

Swift devastation: this is what a storm brings! When it does, we all want immediate relief. The storm itself only lasts a little while; it's the aftermath that can linger, and if the storm is a severe one, the recovery won't be quick. In order to feel immediate relief from the effects of a storm, you will need to employ some basic survival skills. Through my experiences, I have learned a few of these survival skills, which I will share with you so that you can experience immediate relief after your own storm. I call these skills the "Three B's of Storm Management."

3 B's of Storm Management | B-1: Breathe!

"I can't breathe!" I remember saying when my storm knocked the wind out of me. When my unexpected tragedy hit, it literally took my breath away. There are times when you can go through challenges and manage your pain on the inside without displaying any visible effects of the pain externally. Then, there are those times when you are so gripped by the pain that you are feeling inside that you experience unusual manifestations in your body, pain so intense that you even begin to physically manifest the effects of the pain to the outside world. Try as you may, you simply cannot hide it.

In the midst of such devastating pain, there will be times when you are doing really well just to manage to breathe... and that's okay! The pain and shock of a trauma can be paralyzing. The more we think about our circumstances, the more we can become overwhelmed with grief, helplessness and even panic – so much so that we cannot breathe. In fact, you may be so overcome with your painful situation that you think to yourself, *I don't want to breathe!* This is understandable, because breathing allows the reality of the tragedy to settle into your spirit – something that you may try to avoid at any cost. As hard as it seems to move on to this acceptance of reality, you must do it; take the first step by taking that breath. My encouragement to you is to accept what has happened in your storm and then *choose* to breathe!

Genesis 2:7 says *"And the Lord God formed man from the dust of the ground, and breathed into his nostrils the breath of life, and the man became a living being."* God is the giver of breath and life. The Word of God provides life to your soul. Breathing also illustrates our human vulnerability and complete dependence upon God, because we cannot breathe without Him!

Here's an exercise: Try holding your breath right now. How long did it take before your chest started to ache? How well were you able to function once you ran out of breath? The answers to these questions should remind you that breathing is absolutely necessary to sustain us from moment to moment!

A friend of mine was heavily involved in yoga, and she would often stop by my office to share how it could be helpful for managing stress and for sleeping better at night. Out of a "sudden curiosity" (or so I thought), I started taking yoga classes.

One of the first things that I learned was breathing techniques. Yoga taught me how to breathe slowly and deliberately in a way that relaxes and de-stresses the body.

After leaving my class one Saturday morning in December, my phone rang, and it was A.J. I told him that I was leaving my yoga class, and he blurted out, "I am taking yoga too, and I love it!" We talked about the various positions and how difficult they were. We agreed to eventually take a class together.

Looking back, God knew that this storm would knock the wind out of me for a while and that I would need some special training to avoid hyperventilating. I would need to learn how to breathe with a purpose. In times of tragedy, we should breathe with a purpose. Breathe in God's Word and breathe out (let go of) any negative thoughts, pain, fear or grief. You must intentionally take in life with each breath. The scripture says in Deuteronomy 30:19 *"...I have set before you life and death, blessing and cursing, now choose life..."* Choosing to breathe means choosing life!

> **Breathe in:** *"Sustain me, My God, according to Your promise, and I will live..."* (Psalm 119:116)
> **Breathe out:** "I can't go on any longer."
>
> **Breathe in:** *"For I know the plans I have for you declares the Lord... plans to give you a future and a hope."* (Jeremiah 29:11)
> **Breathe out:** "Why did this happen?"
>
> **Breathe in:** *"I can do all things through Him that gives me strength."* (Philippians 4:13)
> **Breathe out:** "This is too hard."
>
> **Breathe in:** *"And we know that in all things, God works for the good of those who love Him, who have been called according to His purpose."* (Romans 8:28)

Breathe out: "Things will never work out."

On several occasions, my response to people who would ask me how I was doing was, "I am just trying to *breathe* right now!" I know that they did not understand how literal that statement was to me, but it was very true.

Whenever your circumstances begin to overwhelm you, stop where you are and breathe very intentionally. Every breath you take is from your Almighty God. With each breath, you will feel your physical body start to relax. Then, you will be able to move forward for a little while longer. Breathe with a deliberate purpose as often as needed. To quote author Sharon Williams, "Breathe, baby, *breathe!*"

3 B's of Storm Management | B-2: Be!

Sometimes, "pleasant pretending" is necessary. You know, those times when things may not be going well and yet you make a conscious effort to be pleasant for the sake of those around you. During such seasons, you simply will yourself to smile politely until times get better. However, when you are in the midst of a major storm, there's simply no time for "pleasant pretending"! In fact, during these times, pretending will lead to a major disaster later on, so it's best to just allow yourself to "be" during these times of hardship! Be whom? Be who you are, Be how you feel, Be where you are, Be honest with yourself, Be honest with God and Be ready for a change!

Psalm 139:1-4 says, *"You have searched me, Lord, and You know me. You know when I sit and when I rise; You perceive my thoughts from afar. You discern my going out and my lying down; You are familiar with all of my ways. Before a word is on my tongue, You, Lord know it completely."* This helps us to understand that God already knows what is happening in your life, and most importantly, He knows what the outcome will be! After all is said and done, He knows who, what and how you will be as a result of the storm you have weathered. God's Word tells us in Romans 8:28 that *all things* (even storms!) are working together for our good, so we know that what we will be in the end is greater than what we were before the storm arrived!

One of the things that people who go through devastating experiences will often be is emotional. This is not a bad thing, because God made you with all of the emotions that you possess; thus, He is not surprised when certain situations in life activate them and you react in an emotional manner. Believe it or not, God is big enough to handle any emotional reaction you may have in the midst of your storm.

Never be afraid to express your emotions when you are going through, because they are natural responses that help us to cope with the experiences that we encounter in life – good and bad. There is no guidebook that dictates how you are supposed to respond when you are going through a difficult situation, so do not allow the subjective opinions and expectations of others to determine how you should respond to your personal experience. After all, no matter how much people want to see you better, it is difficult to put on a happy face when you are sad and dealing with devastation. It is difficult to have an upbeat, meaningful conversation when you can't breathe. To pretend to be in a place emotionally that you are not for the sake of other people only opens the door for an emotional ambush (an all-of-a-sudden uncontrollable flood of emotions) when you least expect it.

Here's my best advice to you: instead of pretending, just "Be" in the moment. Wherever you are emotionally at any given time, it is what it is until God changes you! Therefore, if you don't *feel like* picking up the phone when it rings, don't pick it up. If you don't *feel like* responding to an e-mail, don't respond. If you don't *feel like* having visitors, don't open the door. If you are having a good day, *enjoy* it. If you have laughter in your soul, *laugh*. If you *feel* strong enough to take on a project, take it on. You will quickly find out that the world continues to move forward while you take time to "Be." Take time to be yourself in the early moments of your storm. Be imperfect, be flawed, be confused and be broken. It's all a part of the process.

God changes people, situations and things for His glory in His own time; nothing changes overnight. This process of continual change is referred to as "becoming," and it is only God who can make you to "become" in the midst of a storm. What's more, He will not judge you during your process of becoming, so feel the freedom to share your raw emotions fully with God. If you are fortunate enough to have a close friend who will listen, share with them also, as long as they will allow you to freely express yourself without giving you directives and timelines on how you should feel and behave.

A word of caution: if a well-meaning and loving person in your life begins a word of advice with "You need to...," "Why don't you...," or "If I were you...," listen politely, thank them, smile and simply walk away. Allow yourself to just "Be" until God changes things. Everyone may not understand you or agree with your actions or attitudes, but let no one stand in the way of your healing. Do what *you* have to do to get better in *your* own way. If it is your heart's desire to get past your storm, God will deliver you in due season.

The righteous cry for help, and the Lord hears them; He delivers them from all their troubles. The Lord is close to the brokenhearted and saves those who are crushed in spirit. The righteous person may have many troubles, but the Lord delivers him from them all. Psalm 34:17-19

3 B's of Storm Management | **B-3: Bow!**

The third thing that you should do to experience some immediate relief from the storm is surrender! Let it go! Why? Because you can't change a thing! For those of us who are "fixers," something will eventually happen that you cannot fix. The faster we understand that only God has total control and that all we can do is simply "Bow" down and surrender to His sovereignty, the better. To surrender does not mean that you are giving up; it just means that you are going in a different direction – the direction that God has allowed.

There is an awesome freedom when we simply bow down to God's will and "allow" Him to be responsible for the outcome. As a known "fixer," I had to come to my own understanding about this, accepting the fact that I don't know anything, I can't do anything on my own, and I have no power over anything. It's quite a humbling realization... and a *freeing* one! To be able to say "This is Yours, God. I don't know anything. You are running the show, and I am just here!" is quite liberating!

Sometimes we tend to feel that we should be exempt from tragedy – that it should happen to people who "deserve it" instead of us. However, who actually *deserves* to experience tragedy? Regardless of who they are, how they are, or where they live, *everyone* in this world will experience tragic situations in their lifetime. When a storm hits a community, it does not skip over the homes of "good people," nor does it target the homes of "bad people." Like the scripture says in Matthew 5:45, God sends rain on the just and the unjust alike. In light of this, regardless of whether you think you "deserve" your storm or not, accept it, bow down to the One who calms the raging winds and rain, and allow Him to give you peace in the midst of it.

Once the Storm Has Arrived: Things to Consider

If an unexpected storm has arrived in your life, understand that God knows about it, and He cares about you. He is neither a respecter of persons nor a respecter of storm size, so regardless of who you are or what you are going through, the details of your life are just as important to God as those of another person.

When the storm arrives, breathe, be and bow. I will warn you that doing these things will not be easy, especially when you are doing everything you can to just try to make it through the day; however, they do work. You must believe that trusting in God will help you get through the early stages of your storm. The pain will not simply go away, but you will at least be able to get through each day, one day at a time.

As you walk through your storm, also remember that things will not be clear. However, in the midst of the fog, expect to see glimpses of God working on your behalf to see you through. These *Flashes in the Fog* will give you hope, strength and confirmation that despite your storm, you are not alone, and you are loved by God.

We don't yet see things clearly.
We're squinting in a fog, peering through a mist.

But it won't be long before the weather clears and the sun shines bright! We'll see it all then, see it all as clearly as God sees us, knowing Him directly just as He knows us!
1 Corinthians 13:12 (The Message)

Arlener Steels-Poydras

2
ZERO VISIBILITY (I CAN'T SEE!)

Squinting through the Storm: Can You See It?

One of the things that always makes me laugh is watching television reporters during a major storm, especially a hurricane. They stand out in the middle of the severe weather, attempting to deliver a news story to the viewers who are watching safely and soundly from the warm, dry comfort of their homes. Winds are blowing more than 60 - 90 miles per hour, rain is coming down by the bucketful, flood waters are up to their knees, and there the reporters are yelling into a microphone to report to us how harsh the weather is! Watching them as they try to maintain their footing, hold on for dear life and try to keep from being blown away by the strong winds is the hilarious part!

During these special reports, one of the things that I always observe is that the reporters' visibility is greatly impaired as they struggle to see through the angry winds and rain. Throughout their entire segment, they can be seen squinting and shielding their eyes from the storm as they try to deliver their report for the camera. Likewise, when the storms of life rage around you, it is difficult to see your way out.

A violent storm usually brings darkness, heavy rain and wind. Sometimes, the winds blow so hard that you must close your eyes and shield your face to protect yourself from debris. Your vision is obstructed, and you cannot see through your storm! While we know that life must go on and that our normal daily activities must continue to occur, during a storm, we are often in such a mental fog that clearly seeing and understanding what is happening around us seems nearly impossible. It is only by the grace of God that we somehow manage to complete our daily tasks and meet our daily needs while learning to walk through the fog with such restricted vision.

Another area in which our vision can be restricted is in the area of hope: you don't know if your life can be put back together after the devastation left by the storm, because you just can't see it happening – hope is nowhere in view. The divorce papers are already signed, the bankruptcy has already been filed, the leg has already been amputated, your last day of work was today, the disease has already been confirmed, or your hope of having children has already been dashed by the doctor's report.

Everything seems to be such an inevitable "done deal" that you can't see anything different happening. However, even though you cannot always see Him, God is right there in the middle of the storm with you, making His presence known by sending *Flashes in the Fog*. These flashes are designed to provide you with the hope that He is in full control of the situation, and it's not over until *He* says it is over!

Following the Flashes:
Seeing a Sovereign God through the Fog

As a fog of hopelessness, depression, confusion, and disappointment overshadowed my life and obscured my vision, I immediately went searching for the *Why's*. The events (which I call *Flashes in the Fog*) that I chronicled while I was in the fog are my personal experiences and testimonies of how God is there in the midst of the fog, unseen, but orchestrating the events of your life as He sees fit. I share my specific examples of the flashes that He showed me so that you can see just how intimately God is connected to us and our lives, down to the tiniest details. To speak about His participation in our lives in general terms would not do the principle justice. Only by sharing the intimate details of my experiences with Him during my storm will you be able to understand just how much He truly cares about everything that concerns us.

I also share a few of my *Flashes in the Fog* to give you the hope that the mighty hand of God reaches out into the mundane details of our lives in order to lovingly show us that He is God. These little flashes are what a non-believer would call 'coincidence,' 'karma' or 'happenstance.' However as a Christian, I clearly understand that these incidents were clearly the hand of God moving in my life in the midst of my storm.

While in the storm, I had to choose to believe that the God I worship is in control of all things – even those things that I did not understand. This makes me a "non-understanding believer," and I am just fine with that! Because God is sovereign, whatever He wants me to know or see, He will reveal – even in the fog.

God is sovereign, which means that He can do or allow whatever He wants, whenever He wants, and however He wants. He is God! God is also omniscient, so He knows exactly what is happening to you at all times! He is never caught off guard with anything that has occurred in your life. In fact, not only does He know about what is happening in your life, He has personally *allowed* it! Therefore, God knows, and God controls. Making a conscious choice to accept that God is sovereign and controls this entire universe, even down to the minute details of your life, will set you free!

This notion may cause some to instantly panic, but not those who choose to stand on what God's Word says in Romans 8:28: *"And we know that in all things God works for the good of those who love Him and have been called according to His purpose."* "All things" means *all* things – including the storms of life!

When we are trying to weather some of the darkest storms of our lives, praying that God would deliver us out of them, but seemingly to no avail, we can be tempted to ask questions like *"Does God really care about me? Does God really know what I'm going through?"* Rest assured, He knows *and* He cares. This is the very reason why He allows us to see *Flashes in the Fog*! These flashes of light, glimpses of grace, and lessons of love that we experience in the fog encourage us as we go through the darkness.

I like to think of these flashes as "Holy Hugs" that are designed to leave an indelible mark upon our lives – lasting impressions from the storm. Seeing the right flash at the right time can make you drop your jaw in amazement, smile through tears and even laugh out loud. These

Flashes in the Fog can be so specifically tailored to your immediate need that you know without a shadow of a doubt that God is right in the midst of your darkness, increasing your visibility of Him!

During my storm, my visibility was zero. I could not see my way in any direction. I could not see hope anywhere I looked. However, God met me right where I was and used everyday things to make His presence clearly known and felt by me. He was not only there *with* me; He was doing some of His best work *in* me! Transformation often occurs even as we are walking through the midst of a dark fog.

What's In a Song:
Trusting in Jesus to Deliver

On November 10, 2011, my sister, Lawanda Steels, passed away at the age of 45. At her hospital bedside were my son A.J., my husband Lumus and myself. On the CD player in her room, we played one of my favorite songs, *Trust In Jesus*, and it permeated throughout the Intensive Care Unit of the hospital. As we opened the curtain to exit her room, the ICU staff was listening through their tears.

My sister had been ill and unresponsive for several

months, so we were not surprised when she finally passed away peacefully. When things happen that are outside of our control and without warning, they are difficult to accept. However, there is a marked difference between things for which we have been given an opportunity to prepare because we have advance notice versus tragedies that strike suddenly without any warning. The latter are the ones that really test the faith.

On February 20, 2012, when my only son died, I railed at God – yes, I did! I was distraught, confused, angry and devastated. When our pastor arrived at our home to counsel and comfort us, we gathered in the living area for prayer. Even as he prayed, I continued saying, *"It can't be true. It can't be true. Why did this happen?"* To God, I said, *"You promised to deliver A.J."* Then, just as our pastor finished his prayer, my husband whispered into my ear, "He *did* deliver him."

Just as my husband whispered in my ear,
reminding me that A.J. had indeed been
delivered, I heard the Christian radio station

playing in the background. The song that played: Trust In Jesus.

Noticing this, I said aloud, "That's the song that was playing when Lawanda passed." Then a still small voice whispered in my ear, "If I'm good enough for your sister, I'm good enough for your son. Trust in Jesus."

There in the midst of my tears, I felt an unexplainable peace despite my pain. God knew in advance! It is so comforting to know that God loves us and is close to us, even when tragedies occur. Hearing that same song at that exact time let me know that God still loved me in spite of what He had allowed to happen in my world!

Revelation 1:18 says that *"Jesus holds all the keys to life and death. So everyone's departure rests in His hands."* This revelation brings peace to my heart. I imagine Jesus standing before me holding the keys to life and death and assuring me, *"Don't be afraid. I hold all of the keys."* Therefore, my response is like that of Job which says, *"The Lord gave, and the Lord has taken away, may the name of the Lord be praised"* (Job 1:21).

God is in control of all things and rules over all things. He has power and authority over nature, earthly kings, history, angels, demons and life and death. Even Satan has to ask God's permission before he can act (Psalm 103:19). This gives us even more reason to trust our sovereign God and what He allows to happen in our lives. Although my understanding, visibility and hope during the time of my storm were zero, and although I could not see my way even through the next few seconds of my life, God gave me hope by gently reminding me through a simple song that I should continue to trust in Jesus. God made Himself visible to me by using a *simple song*!

A Sense of Humor:
Angels in the Strangest of Places!

The week following A.J.'s homegoing celebration, the simplest things became difficult for me. Within seconds of starting to do something, I could not remember what I was doing. In the midst of a sentence, I would forget what I was saying. As I drove in my car, I even forgot where I was going. This was life in the middle of the dark fog. Getting from one destination to another was difficult for me. I even recall one incident in which I went to the grocery store and could not find my keys, my wallet... nothing. My husband Lumus had to come and get me from the store. This was the day that he began "Driving Ms. Arlener." He drove me to work, to church and anywhere else I needed to go. Oftentimes, Lumus and I would just get into the car and drive with no particular destination in mind.

Looking back on that season, I have to laugh! God not only had a sense of humor, but also He had a purpose for the grocery store incident that led to this season during which my husband had to chauffeur me around. You see, as Lumus would drive, he would also preach *non-stop*! I remember uttering the silent prayer, "Lord, I *really do* believe. I *promise* I do! Can you *please* tell him to stop preaching?" Despite my silent pleas, Lumus continued to preach. Sometimes, I even wanted to give an offering (*giggle*)! However, in all seriousness, the Word spoken by him during these times was God's way of getting His Word into my heart. I had neither the strength nor the concentration in those early days of the storm to read the Bible, so God gave me the Bible via audio... through my husband!

The Word says in Psalm 139:7-9, *"Where can I flee from Your presence? If I go up to the heavens, You are there; if I make my bed in the depths, You are there. If I rise on the wings of the dawn, if I settle on the far side of the sea, even there Your hand would guide me, Your right hand shall hold me fast. If I were to say, 'Certainly the darkness will cover me, and the light will turn to night all around me', even the darkness is not too dark for You to see, and the night is as bright as day; darkness and light are the same to You."* I lived the truth of this scripture as my husband and I wandered around in a dark fog the week after A.J.'s funeral. God saw our every move and knew our deep sadness. However, the darkness was not dark to Him, and He wanted to make us smile, even in the fog.

After eating lunch one afternoon, I told my husband that I wanted a glass of wine, thinking that it would make the hurt go away. He agreed, and off we went. The store was more than 15 miles from our home. *Funny*, I remember thinking to myself, *The preacher and his wife going out of the way so that they won't be seen by people who think that Christians can't have a drink!*

As we pulled up to the liquor store, I noticed a very nice baby blue convertible Mercedes parked out front. An elderly man with white hair was sitting in the car. As we pulled into the parking lot, he was getting out of the car and walking into the store. I remember thinking to myself, *Nice car*, because it was the perfect weather for a convertible.

My husband went into the store while I sat in the car. Several minutes later, my husband emerged carrying our bag with a stunned look on his face. My initial thought was that the store had been robbed or that something terrible had happened inside. When he got into the car, he said, "You are not going to believe me, so I will just back out and drive really slowly."

As he was backing out, I asked him, "What are you talking about?" Just then, as we passed the convertible Mercedes, the elderly man was getting into his own car.

My husband pointed at him and said, "That man just paid for our stuff!" As he was pointing, the man began to walk towards our car, so Lumus let my window down on the passenger's side. I put my hand out the window of the car with the intention of shaking his hand.

The elderly man put his hand on top of my hand. As he looked at me with crystal blue eyes, he said, "God told me to tell you that He knows what He is doing and that it's going to be alright."

Tears began to roll down my face. Then, the man simply said, "God bless you" and walked away. I looked over at Lumus in amazement as we drove away with tears in our eyes.

There is no doubt in my mind that this man was on assignment by my God! God made Himself visible to us through a complete stranger! God can communicate to us any way He chooses, using anyone and anything He chooses, because He is God. Hebrews 13:2 says, *"Do not forget to show hospitality to strangers, for by so doing, some people have shown hospitality to angels without knowing."* God loves us and knows exactly where we are and what we need. He dispatched an angel to a liquor store to tell the Preacher and his wife that He is still God, and He still cares for us. My eyes were opened again in that very moment, and my vision was crystal clear, even in the fog. God is sovereign and loving, and He definitely has a sense of humor!

Timing Is Everything... Even in Private Time!

On March 10th, a Saturday afternoon, my husband had been watching sports and had fallen asleep in front of the television. I thought to myself, *This is the perfect time. I can go upstairs and go through A.J.'s things in private.* I climbed the stairs, walked into his room, and settled in for the task before me.

I started by pulling open a box of books. As I began to thumb through the pages, I noticed that he had written several funny notes, and I chuckled as I read them. I marveled over his original artwork that filled the room; he was an exceptional artist. Then, I began to think about the fact that his birthday would have been in six days, and we would not be able to celebrate it. My eyes filled with tears. All at once, I became overwhelmed with depression. This was it: I was about to have a private pity party.

Tragedies and storms have a way of bringing out the multiple personalities in all of us; we can go from laughter to tears at any given moment. As I stood in the middle of the room, I became very weak. I sat down on the floor, overwhelmed with sadness and depression.

At that very moment (4:45 p.m.), a text message came from Lynn Turner. It said, *"May God strengthen you today is my prayer. We bind depression right now and lift up the name of Jesus. Know that I'm thinking about you and just lifted you before the Lord. Love you. Be blessed!"*

I sent her a text back and said, *"How did you know I was sitting on the floor crying unless God told you? Thank you, Jesus."*
She said, *"I thank God I was obedient to His voice. Try to think of something that will make you cry funny tears!"*
I responded, *"Thanks, Lynn! I got up and started cleaning. Thank you so much!"*

I have known Lynn for years as a distant associate; we might have seen each other twice a year. When her text message came in, I initially thought, *Lynn is texting me? Something must be wrong.* I opened the text only to find a message from God!

God knew that the text had to come from someone whom I rarely communicated with in order to get my attention. When I read the message, I felt like God was right there on that floor crying with me, and He used Lynn to send me a message to remind me that He is sovereign and sees my struggle.

The still small voice inside of me said, "Get up, lil' girl!" I got up off of the floor and went on a cleaning spree. I did A.J.'s laundry, sorted the things to give away, and thanked God for the 23 years that I'd had him.

My husband had begun purchasing Willow Tree statues for me many years before. He would probably buy one or two a year, so I had a small collection, not quite up to 10 yet. I placed them around family pictures on the dresser in our bedroom. Sitting there looking at them one day after my storm, I said, "I don't want any more of these. We should start something new."

A Flash in the FOG

When the mail came a couple of days later, there was a package for me. I was surprised to see that it was from Marce Graham, a lady I had worked with more than 23 years ago. I opened it and was shocked to find a Willow Tree statue of a little boy holding a bronze heart. I quickly went to my bedroom to look at my collections and I did NOT have that one! I smiled and said to myself, God loves me.

Marce and I might have had lunch or dinner 5 times or so in those 23 years since we had worked together. We might have spoken with each other once or twice a year. I picked up the phone and called her. She said that she had heard the news about A.J. I asked her how she knew I collected Willow Tree statues. She said, "I don't know why I picked that statue. I had never heard of them before. I went out at lunch one day and was looking around for something special, and it caught my eye." We were both amazed at what God had done!

God is there even in the midst of our private times; He knows where we are, what we are doing and what we need. God knows who we are and how we are because He made us in His image. In the same way that He was with me, God will be with you in your private moments. Whether they are temper tantrums, fits of rage, laughter or uncontrollable tears, He is there. Although our "private" times are private to us, God will make Himself visible right in the middle of them!

Daily Bread & Devotionals:
What a Difference a Year Makes!

I received a gift in April 2011 from my secret sister, Pam Daniels. It was a one-year *My Daily Bread* devotional book. I started reading it as part of my morning quiet time and using it as a journal. It was a source of information and inspiration at just the right time during that year.

After A.J. passed away, I would sporadically read a page from the devotional. In my storm, I had gotten off track from having my regular devotional period each day. I went several weeks, from March 21st to April 23rd, without reading or writing anything. My new reality had set in, and I was broken and discouraged, trying to navigate my way through the dark fog.

On April 23, 2012, I felt the urge to get back on track with my daily devotional reading. When I opened the book to the April 23, 2012 reading at 2:30 a.m., I saw that this was the EXACT date I had started reading and writing in the book one year prior on April 23, 2011! The scripture for that day in 2011 was 2 Corinthians 5:8: *"We are confident, I say, and would prefer to be away from the body and at home with the Lord."* The commentary of that scripture described death as a person who has passed from this life and is sailing off into the ocean. Friends and loved ones on the shore are waving goodbye and saying how much they will miss them as they sail away, while on the opposite shore, people are beckoning to them with excitement, anticipating their arrival and welcoming them with smiles and great joy!

And there it was, in my own handwriting. Exactly one year earlier to the date, I had written: "Heaven is real, and God promises us another body. Just know and comfort others who don't know. I pray that I am able to hold

this in my heart and use it when my turn comes."

I smiled through my tears at how God had used His Word and then my own words in my own writing to comfort me in the middle of the night. Yet again, God met me where I was and reminded me of His sovereignty and love for me. A year earlier, He had orchestrated events in such a way that I would be able to look back and see Him clearly, even in the fog.

When you are going through difficult times, you might tend to question your thoughts and what you see. You might second-guess everything, and sometimes you might even doubt God. Thoughts from the enemy (Satan) would have you doubt that God is interested in or concerned about you; he would rather you believe that God has abandoned you so that you begin to feel hopeless, desperate and abandoned. Further, the enemy would have you to believe that if and when God shows up through *Flashes in the Fog* in the ways He did for me, these are just coincidences, not messages from God or visitations from the Lord. In fact, Satan would have you question and doubt whether various parts of this book that you are reading – *my* story – are factual or fabricated!

Fortunately, God knows that we are prone to such attacks in the mind during difficult times. He knows our skepticism and the questions that we will ask as we try to make our way through the storm. I am no different; I had my doubts, too! However, just to show me that He was merciful and close to the brokenhearted, God sent yet another confirmation that said to me, *"Yes, I am God, and I am here! Believe that!"*

As I was getting ready for work the very next morning (April 23, 2012), I received a text message from a friend, Meloda Clayton. It was 6:58 a.m. The text message said: "It's just a temporary separation. The next time you get together, it will be forever. To be absent from the body is to be present with the Lord."

I almost dropped my cell phone as I looked around anxiously. Then I laughed out loud and said, "Thank you, Jesus!" God was saying specifically to me, "I know how hard-headed you are lil' girl! Just sending you a confirmation of what I said to you at 2:30 a.m. this morning!"

He *Sees* You, But You Must *Know* Him!

What are you going through right now? It is possible that your visibility in your situation might be zero, and you cannot possibly see your way clear or see anything good coming out of this storm. However, know this: God sees, and God cares!

In the midst of your situation, make a conscious effort to look for glimpses of God in your darkest times, because He is there for those who believe! During the months after my storm, God met me wherever I was and used *Flashes in the Fog* to comfort and reassure me that He was there. God can do the same things for you that He did for me; however, you will not be able to recognize Him if you do not first *know* Him. If God asked you right now, *"Why should I let you into heaven?"* what would your answer be?

The Bible says in Acts 16:31 *"Believe on the Lord Jesus Christ and you will be saved, you and your household."* You have to believe that Jesus Christ is the Son of God, that He died for your sins, and that He was raised from the grave so that you might have eternal life. Confessing and believing this places you in a covenant relationship with God.

In God's Word, Hebrews 13:5, He has promised you that He will never leave you nor forsake you. In His Word, there are promises made only to those who believe in Him through His Son Jesus Christ. Even if you don't understand why life is the way it is, why the world operates like it does, or even why God chooses to do what He does, be a "non-understanding believer" in Jesus Christ. Then when you get to heaven, you will understand!

It is my prayer that as a believer in Jesus Christ, you know that I am no more special to God than you are! He loves us all equally. No matter what we go through, God loves us. You must *look for Him* in the midst of your darkest days because *He is there* with you in the fog, wanting so very much to lead you out of it. Sincerely look for Him through the eyes of your heart, and you *will* see Him.

Although you might have zero visibility right now and cannot see yourself on the other side of your situation, God sees all and He knows all. Allow Him to show His concern for you by using people, places and things to encourage you. He will give you peace and will to continue to reveal Himself to you through the little flashes of hope – *Flashes in the Fog*. The Bible says in Job 29:3, "*By His light I walked through the darkness...*" God always has 100% visibility, even during a storm!

3
STORM CHASING

Changing the Game:
Taking the Storm by the Horns

One of my favorite movies is *Twister*. Until I saw this movie, I did not realize that there were people who actually chased storms for a living! Once they tracked a storm, they would drive directly into the storm's path and attempt to gather data about the storm's attributes. Then, they would use the data to determine the storm's severity and to help predict future storms.

However, there was one thing that they could not do: stop the storm. Thus, once they set up their equipment, they would take cover and watch it pass, hoping that they made it out alive. Each time they made it through the storm and came out alive, they were exhilarated! This made no sense to me – back then, that is! Today, I have a different perspective.

I could not stop the storm that came into my life. Almost one year later, I do not have ample words to express my amazement that I am still here, functioning, joyful and better than I was before the storm! It makes absolutely no sense! Since I could do nothing about what had happened, I decided to lean into it head-on by going after my storm in some very specific ways. In other words, I became a storm chaser!

As each month following your storm passes, the harsh reality of your situation will settle in, and you will eventually arrive at a cold and crippling "new normal." I believe that God uses shock to get us through the toughest times, and then, by the time the shock wears off, we are through the initial stage of the storm. In your case, while the initial shock of your storm might have worn off, the remnants are still painfully impacting your life. For example, you might *still* be going through a divorce, you might *still* be unemployed after being laid off, your reputation might *still* be damaged, the cancer might *still* not be in remission, you might *still* be in financial ruin, you might *still* be unable to have children... and as for me, my son was *still* dead.

Despite having to continually deal with the lasting effects of the storm, I was encouraged by the *Flashes in the Fog* that I know came from a loving God. These flashes drove me to aggressively chase after my storm. Instead of wishing it had never happened, attempting to forget that it had happened, or desperately trying to focus on happier times, I made a conscious decision to allow the waves of my storm to wash over me in every way.

I realized that taking a passive approach and waiting on a miraculous answer to take away my pain was not the right path for me. Instead of denying what had happened and running from reality, I decided to chase down my pain and walk through it face forward as though walking through a blizzard. I decided to chase my storm instead of allowing my storm to chase me. When I allowed myself to embrace the harsh reality of my situation, I began a rollercoaster ride of uncontrollable emotions.

As I began to chase my storm, I had hopes that it would pass more quickly. However, instead, I found myself covered in what I now call the "Divine Darkness." The scripture says in 1 Kings 8:22, *"The Lord said that He will dwell in a dark cloud."* After my storm, I experienced the truth of this scripture. It was there in the dark that God met me and equipped me to get through each and every day.

Like professional storm chasers that come well-equipped with the necessary tools and resources to chase their storms in the natural, there are also spiritual tools that we must equip ourselves with as we prepare to chase the painful storms of our lives. The two primary tools that you will need to chase a storm include the Word of God and worship.

Tools of the Storm Chasers:
The Word of God and Worship

Storm Chaser Tool 1 | **The Word of God**

Like any Christian, I have always had my favorite verses in the Bible that I would use to encourage myself. For example, Psalm 37:4 is one of my favorites, as it says, *"Take delight in the Lord, and He will give you the desires of your heart."* However, during this time, instead of taking the scripture at face value to mean what I had always known it to mean in my life, I asked myself, *How does this fit into my life now? How is He giving me the desire of my heart by allowing my son to be gone?*

Despite these questions, there were two things that I held onto as firm beliefs: 1) I know that God is good; 2) If God said it, then it *must* be true. God does not lie, so if there seems to be a contradiction between what the Scriptures say and what I experience, I know that it is my understanding that is off, not the Scriptures. Thus, I realized that I needed to dig beneath the surface to discover what this verse meant in its original context.

I learned that, taken in the proper context, this scripture tells the righteous not to envy the prosperity of the wicked, because the wicked will soon fade away. Contrary to popular misinterpretation, this scripture is not a promise that God will give me whatever I want as long as I think positive thoughts about Him. The deeper I searched through the context of this scripture, the more I discovered about God's character, His love and His desire for me. I also realized that my ultimate heart's desire was still for God alone. As I delighted myself in the Lord, He became my *only* delight and my *only* desire.

As I chased my storm, I had many favorite scriptures that I had to go back and examine in the same way for their true meanings. In order to effectively use the Word of God as we chase our storms, we must use the Word according to its intended meaning, which can only be understood when we examine it in its proper context. Otherwise, we might be using this tool in a way that was completely unintended by the Author, resulting in its ineffectiveness!

In the early days after A.J.'s death, my home was full of people. They brought conversation, hugs, tears, food, advice and inquisitive personalities. As with any situation, people will be compelled to come and provide support and advice. Being a private person, I would often quietly disappear into my bedroom with a quick, "I'll be right back." I would go into my bedroom, close the door, then go into the bathroom, close the door, then go into the closet and close that door. In the dark, I would grab a pillow, place it over my face and scream for several minutes. Afterwards, I would wash my face, comb my hair and return to my guests to visit for a little while longer. I would repeat this process several times a day as people continued to come.

It was dark and quiet in that closet where no one could see or hear my pain... or so I thought. Four months later, I would again find myself sitting in the dark alone with my thoughts. Escaping to a dark and quiet place became a peaceful time of cleansing, prayer and healing. In my own words, I recall saying, *"My faith is broken."* Little did I know that as I sat in my spiritual darkness in the midst of my dark closet, this was the very place where God was planning a "faith makeover" just for me.

My experience had always been to read God's Word to find the answers to life's questions. The difference this time was that a storm of epic proportions had devastated me. As a result, I was too weak and distraught to know where to start reading. Thus, I just picked up my Bible and started aimlessly reading at the beginning... or so I *thought* it was aimless!

Genesis 1:2 says, "Now the earth was formless and empty, darkness was over the surface of the deep, and the Spirit of God was hovering over the waters."

Before I could get past this verse, the still small voice within me started to speak. It said, "If I can create the world out of darkness, surely I can handle your broken faith, lil' girl." I smiled! God can meet you just where you are, even if you are in the dark and cannot find your way out.

When I sought to become a storm chaser, I thought that I was chasing my storm by acknowledging my pain and facing it head on. In actuality, as I began my chase, I soon realized that I was not chasing the pain; I was chasing the One who owns the storm and who can absolutely calm the storm by His powerful hand!

As a storm chaser, I began a different kind of journey through God's Word, searching for answers to my questions. In all my years of reading the Bible, I had read the story of Job many times. However, I had never noticed the words at the beginning of chapter 38 before. They read *"And God answered Job from the eye of a violent storm"* (The Message). With all of the tragedies that befell Job, His losses made my loss seem small and insignificant by comparison. However, to me, my storm was the most important thing in the world because it was *my* storm – a storm that directly impacted *me* in a major way. In this, I realized that my personal storm story would never be as impactful to others as it was to me. In the same fashion, others' storm stories (no matter what they are) are the biggest and most important things in *their* world, because they are personal for *them*.

Storms are very close, very personal experiences whose strength and magnitude can only be measured by those who experience a direct hit from them. Anyone else is simply a bystander, like those who watch the storm report from the warmth and comfort of their couches, and they will never be able to comprehend the first-hand devastation and raw pain that you experience in the middle of your own storm. They can empathize with you or even sympathize with you if they have gone through a similar storm. They can feel a sense of pain, but their pain is not the pain that you feel; their pain is a byproduct of seeing you, someone whom they love, in pain, while your pain comes from experiencing the direct impact of the storm's devastation. There is a difference. In light of this, to expect others to feel the true brunt of your storm's impact as a bystander is unrealistic.

For example, I am reminded of a lady who was sharing the story of her own storm with me. She had been depressed and crying uncontrollably for weeks because she had been accustomed to either talking with her son on the phone every day or having him stop by to see her each week. Now that he was married, her son would only call once in a while. As she told me about her storm, she was talking and crying uncontrollably. To that lady, her storm was her main focus. While I could not feel the impact of her storm as strongly as she could, I did what I *could* do: listen and have empathy.

As I read Job's story, it was not just the tragedies that caught my attention; it was the fact that *"God spoke out of a violent storm."* These few words reassured me that God was in the middle of the storm and was able to speak. The 1996 movie *Twister* has a scene in which a violent tornado hit a small town. There were houses, animals and other debris swirling around in the tornado. However, at the center of the storm, things were completely still. In my mind's eye, I envisioned a storm a million times larger than a category five tornado. The debris in the storm consisted of planets and other heavenly bodies. In the middle of the heavenly tornado, God sat watching as worlds collided. Then, out of the violent storm, He spoke to Job (or to make it personal, *Then, out of the violent storm, God spoke to me!).* God is right in the middle of all of our storms. Not only is He right there with us, but He wants to speak to us through His Word in the middle of the storm!

Applying God's Word to my storm began to strengthen me. The Bible says in Psalm 139:12 that *"even the darkness is as light to God."* I made a renewed commitment to pick up my Bible each day and just read it until times got better. I had nowhere else to turn. Initially, I felt like I was just calling out words as I read. Then, I was led to the book of Psalms where many of my favorite passages were highlighted in my Bible. Most times, I did not see or feel any change as I read. Nonetheless, I would continue to memorize scriptures and recite them all day long just to get through that day. Looking through the Bible one morning, I stumbled (or so I *thought* I had stumbled) across Psalm 116.

At the top of the page where Psalm 116 was found in my Bible was a note in my own handwriting. It said "March 28, 1994, Granny's favorite scripture." My grandmother, Arlener Beverly, passed away on March 28, 1994. She was both

my namesake and my mentor. Her funeral program also contained her favorite scripture, Psalm 116:1: "I love the Lord, He heard my cry..."

I was excited and comforted by God's Word and by memories of my grandmother. Again, that still small voice inside of me said, "This is not about your grandmother, this is for you. These words are for you." I had never before read Psalm 116 in its entirety; I had only read that first verse - my granny's verse.

That day, I read Psalm 116 in its entirety. I began to memorize each section, reciting it every day until all 19 verses were memorized. This passage was specifically speaking to me and my turmoil, so I made it my own:

[1] I love the LORD because He hears my voice and my prayer for mercy.
[2] Because He bends down to listen, I will pray as long as I have breath!
[3] Death wrapped its ropes around me; the terrors of the grave overtook me. I saw only trouble and sorrow.
[4] Then I called on the name of the LORD: "Please, LORD, save me!"
[5] How kind my LORD is! How good He is! So merciful, this God of mine!
[6] The LORD protects those of childlike faith; I was facing death, and He saved me.
[7] Let my soul be at rest again, for the LORD has been good to me.

⁸ He has saved me from death,
my eyes from tears,
my feet from stumbling.
⁹ And so I walk in the LORD's presence
as I live here on earth!
¹⁰ I believed in You, so I said,
"I am deeply troubled, LORD."
¹¹ In my anxiety I cried out to you,
"These people are all liars!"
¹² What can I offer the LORD
for all He has done for me?
¹³ I will lift up the cup of salvation
and praise the LORD's name for saving me.
¹⁴ I will keep my promises to the LORD
in the presence of all His people.
¹⁵ The LORD cares deeply
when His loved ones die.
¹⁶ O LORD, I am Your servant;
yes, I am your servant, born into Your
household;
You have freed me from my chains.
¹⁷ I will offer You a sacrifice of thanksgiving
and call on the name of the LORD.
¹⁸ I will fulfill my vows to the LORD
in the presence of all His people—
¹⁹ in the house of the LORD
in the heart of Jerusalem.
Praise the LORD!
- Psalm 116 (New Living Translation)

Way back in 1994, God knew that in 2012, tragedy was coming to rock my world, and I would be terribly confused and distraught. God knew the way my mind works, so He knew that seeing my grandmother's name in an old Bible would catch my attention. Then, He used this scripture to address my very specific concerns. Each time I read this scripture over several weeks, the small voice inside of me continued to speak specifically to my storm:

- In verses 1 and 2, He confirms that He hears me and even bends down to the floor, where I am, to listen to me.

- Verse 3 communicates my overwhelming thoughts of the grave. Leaving my son at the graveyard was overwhelming. Having already buried my father, sister, grandmother, cousins and aunts, this was a whole new level – one that seemed unnatural.

- Verses 4 to 8 were where I began my chase for answers. I called on the Lord, the only help that I knew. He responded with kindness and mercy. When my son died, I felt like I would die also, but God said "No." He restored my peace and then put my mind and soul at rest again. He assured me that I will walk in His presence for the remainder of my life.

- Verses 10 to 14 express my confusion and anxiety as I cried out to God with my questions. The scripture even expresses my emotion and disappointment at people who view the storms of others as a sport and an opportunity to gossip, embellish stories or simply spread untruths. God's Word covers it all! These verses encouraged me to continue to praise God and do His will.

- Verse 15 is especially dear to my heart. When I recite this scripture, I change the words to say, *"The Lord cares deeply when His A.J. died."* Matthew 10:29 says, *"Not one sparrow falls to the ground apart from the will of God."* God stays close to us, even in death. Believers are precious to God, and He carefully chooses the time when they will be called into His presence. We all have an appointment with death, and only God knows when that time will be. Meanwhile, He is right here with us. This was very comforting to me.

- Verses 16 to 19 remind me of who I am in Christ Jesus and that I must go forward with a sacrifice of praise and service until He calls me home to receive my reward!

Beloved, I went chasing after my storm in the Word of God, and when I did, He gave me specific passages that were just for me. Just as God created something good from the darkness that hovered over the earth, He was able to reshape my faith in Him and set me on a path to new life again. In fact, I rephrased Genesis 1:2 and made it personal: *"Now Arlener was purposeless and empty, darkness was over her life, and the Spirit of God was like living water within her."*

Chase down your storm with God's Word, and you will run right into God in the middle of your storm! He will speak out of the storm and renew your spirit. The closer you get to Him in the center of the storm, the more peace you will experience. Why? Because in the dead center of the storm, there is peace – the place where God can be found!

Storm Chaser Tool 2 | **Worship**

Music can change your mood in an instant. If you put on a sad love song, you will soon find yourself down in the dumps. Conversely, when you are feeling down, just put on your favorite upbeat song and watch the transformation!

As I chased my storm, I surrounded myself with praise and gospel music. I played music while I was in my car, at my job and even when I was exercising – and I played it *loudly*! As the music played, I would always sing along, because for some reason, there is something about turning the music up really loudly that makes you feel like you can sing! Some music brought tears to my eyes as I considered how loving my God was towards me and how much He cared, while other music brought joy as I celebrated all that He had done in my life as well as the great things that were to come. The Psalmist says, "God inhabits the praises of

His people" (Psalm 22:3). God can be found in praise; thus, creating a continual atmosphere of praise was my way of ensuring that God's presence was constantly with me.

Before long, I found myself singing my way out of my storm, and because music also soothes the soul, I found myself to be much more peaceful. While there were times that it took everything in me to utter a word of praise unto God, singing made it easier. It's funny how we will easily sing words that we would not normally say or that we find difficult to express. In the midst of such a trying time, praise was not automatic for me, nor was it easy; it was a choice that took deliberate, intentional effort. It was a sacrifice!

We make sacrifices for people that we really love and things that we really desire. We make sacrifices for our children, our families and even special things that we desire to purchase. Well, Hebrews 13:15 says, *"Through Jesus, therefore, let us continually offer to God a sacrifice of praise – the fruit of our lips that confess His name."* Because I learned how to praise my way through a storm, I now fully understand what it means to bring God a *sacrifice* of praise!

As I weathered my storm, I neither wanted to praise, nor did I feel like praising most of the time. I did not understand why this was, but I so badly wanted God to help me that I was willing to push through my heaviness and burden of grief to praise God, telling Him how awesome and amazing He was through the words of the songs that expressed my sentiments! Looking back over this time, I saw the mighty healing hand of God moving each time I pressed past my pain to praise His holy name! The praise was not only for Him; it was for me, because it continually reminded me of how good my God is!

Another thing that I discovered as I wielded my worship as a tool in chasing my storm was that many songs that were my favorites before February 20th now made me sad. Thus, I went searching for some new songs. One of my co-workers, Wanda Mattox, sat right outside of my office. I believe that God had Wanda on watch duty! She would watch who entered my office, and she would come in and interrupt them with papers in her hand that "needed my signature" when she knew I needed to be rescued so I could be alone. Sometimes, she would simply close my office door (*giggle*)! A discerning spirit knows when another Christian is in distress. Wanda took care of me!

Wanda also sings in her church choir and sent me a link to a praise song that she said would lift my spirits. As soon as I listened to it, I became instantly hooked! It quickly became my new favorite song. The song is *Awesome* by Pastor Charles Jenkins. Even though I can't carry a tune in a bucket, I would sing aloud at the top of my voice each time the song came on, allowing its words and melody to lift my spirits. I felt the closeness of God as I played the song repeatedly, over and over for hours while I worked. The words met me exactly where I was at that time. The lyrics are:

My God is awesome
He can move mountains
Keep me in the valley
Hide me from the rain

My God is awesome
Heals me when I'm broken
Strength where I've been weakened
Forever He will reign

My God is awesome
Savior of the whole world
Giver of salvation
By His stripes I am healed

My God is awesome
Today I am forgiven
His grace is why I'm living
Praise His holy name

I have a special song for my husband and for my daughter, just as I had one for A.J. The song that I had chosen for my son in 2009 and lovingly called "The A.J. song" was *The*

Words I Would Say by Sidewalk Prophets. A.J. knew that this was "his song," and we would often listen to it together. Whenever we were in the car together and it would come on the radio, we would simultaneously say, "It's the A.J. song!" If he would hear it while we were apart, he would call me and say, "My song is playing!" I would do the same, calling him when I heard the familiar tune. As much as I enjoyed this song, however, after my son died, it was one of the songs that made me the saddest; I was unable to listen to it at all after A.J. was gone.

Since A.J.'s death, I had longed to see him, to hear his voice again or just dream about him, but nothing happened. Nothing! One Sunday after church, I fell asleep on the sofa. I was awakened suddenly, so I immediately went upstairs to the guest bedroom.

As I walked into the guest room, A.J. sprang up from under the covers with his huge smile and bright eyes! I remember saying "Hey A.J.! What happened? I've been so sad." He just continued to smile without saying a word. At that moment,

Marie came into the room and yelled, "My A.J.!" I quickly grabbed A.J. by the hand while telling Marie, "Oh, no you're not! You have to wait until I finish!"

I quickly ushered A.J. down the hallway to his bedroom and closed the door. He was still smiling that huge smile without saying one word. Once we were in his room, I began to tell him that I could not listen to the A.J. song anymore because it made me sad. However, I had a new song that I wanted him to hear and told him that he would really like it. He nodded his head, but said nothing. Just smiled. (Remember the smiling for later.)

I grabbed his hand, led him down the hallway, and then headed down the stairs to get my iPhone to play the song Awesome for him. All of a sudden, just as we got to the bottom of the stairs, I woke up! I sat up on the sofa and realized that I had been dreaming. I was so very happy, and I began to thank God that He had allowed me to dream of A.J. and that he was happy! My husband was asleep in the chair, so I attempted to go back to sleep. However, I was so excited that I tossed and turned for a few minutes.

Then, I sat up and picked up my iPhone. On the screen, I saw a red notice indicating that I had a Facebook message. I clicked on the message to see what it was. It was a comment. I could not really make out the face of the person whose picture was in the profile, but I did recognize the name; it was a young lady for whom I had been praying for daily. I thought to myself, That cannot be her. I put my phone back down saying to myself, I will check later. I had finally dreamt about A.J., so I didn't really care about anything else at the moment.

Minutes later, I was prompted to look at the picture again. I still could not make out the face, because the picture was so small on my iPhone. It was at this time that the still small voice inside of me said, "Go upstairs and look on the computer so you can see." I thought to myself, It's no big deal, it's just Facebook. To my thoughts, that small voice answered, "Haven't you been praying for this young lady? Then, go see if it's her."

Finally, after about 20 minutes of debate with myself, I got up off of the sofa and went upstairs to my husband's office to view the picture on the computer. When I got upstairs and sat down at the computer, I was about to click on Facebook when I heard music coming from the small transistor radio that Lumus had left playing on his desk. The radio station was KLTY Christian Radio, and they had just started playing "The A.J. song"!

By the time I was able to focus on the words, the song was playing loud and clear:

Just what I'd say, if we were face to face
I'd tell you just what you mean to me
I'd tell you these simple truths

Be strong in the Lord, never give up hope
You're going to do great things,
I already know
God's got His hand on you,
so don't live life in fear

Forgive and forget,
but don't forget why you're here
Take your time and pray,
thank God for each day
His love will find a way
These are the words I would say

I listened to the entire song for the first time since A.J. died. After the song finished playing, the small voice inside of me said, "Now, all of these years you thought this was 'The A.J. Song', but lil' girl, this song is for you! A.J. is with Me. Take heed to the words of this song, because he is now encouraging you to live on. He is very happy, and you will see him again."

For those who do not believe in Jesus Christ, this means nothing to you. However, let me appeal to your common sense first. What are the chances that I would dream about my son, talk about a specific song, and hear that song playing at the exact time I arrived to hear it? What are the chances that there would be a transistor radio sitting on my husband's desk, already turned on and on the right station? This series of events could not be a mere coincidence! For those who are believers, God is, and God cares about the details of our lives and the storms that we endure, and yes, He can even use music to minister to you at your darkest times.

After that experience, I was able to listen to some of my old favorite songs again. God also introduced me to some new songs that absolutely met me at the point of my pain and lifted me out of the fog. To me, God began to speak out of the storm through Christian music, and this made me want to hear from Him even more.

While listening to Pandora Radio on the internet one day, the song *God Come In* by Zach Neese jumped out at me and became a part of my morning quiet time. It was an open invitation for God to come in and sit with me, which He did through these words:

> *No need for knocking*
> *Come in*
> *More than a guest, You're my friend*
> *You saved my life from the grave*
> *Now it's Yours to take*

These ears are listening
So speak
Your words are like water to me
Cover my soul like the sea
Jesus, rise and fall in me

God come in
Have a seat
I'll lay my crowns and kisses on Your feet
Rise and rest
Friend and King
You are welcome to Your way in me
I adore You

In the early morning hours as I got dressed for work, I would look out of my window at the trees and the sky with the sunlight reflecting off of the pool and listen to these words inviting God into my day. He would always come in, many times through tears, and sometimes through smiles and swaying.

Driving home one day in tears, while listening to listening to KLTY Christian Radio, this wonderful song came over the airways. It was *The Hurt & the Healer* by Mercy Me. The lyrics were:

Flashes in the Fog

Why?
The question that is never far away
The healing doesn't come from the explained
Jesus please don't let this go in vain
You're all I have
All that remains

So here I am
What's left of me
Where glory meets my suffering

I'm alive
Even though a part of me has died
You take my heart and breathe it back to life
I've fallen into Your arms open wide
When the hurt and the Healer collide

Breathe
Sometimes I feel it's all that I can do
Pain so deep that I can hardly move
Just keep my eyes completely fixed on You
Lord take hold and pull me through

So here I am
What's left of me
Where glory meets my suffering

I'm alive
Even though a part of me has died
You take my heart and breathe it back to life
I've fallen into Your arms open wide
When the hurt and the Healer collide

It's the moment when humanity
Is overcome by majesty
When grace is ushered in for good
And all our scars are understood
When mercy takes its rightful place
And all these questions fade away
When out of the weakness we must bow
And hear You say "It's over now"

I'm alive
Even though a part of me has died
You take my heart and breathe it back to life
I've fallen into your arms open wide
When the hurt and the Healer collide

Jesus come and break my fear
Awake my heart and take my tears
Find Your glory even here
When the hurt and the Healer collide

This song tells the story of my grief from beginning to end. Through all of the hurt, it is my desire that God gets glory from me – even in my storm. Nothing else really matters! I boldly went chasing after my storm with worship and praise music, and I collided with the God who was right there in the middle of the storm.

My friend, you have to make a conscious effort to fill your heart with songs of praise and worship. When you cover your storm with praise, things will begin to change: your countenance will be lifted, you will feel closer to God and you will confuse the enemy! One of our greatest weapons of spiritual warfare is praise, so fight back against the attacks of the enemy by exalting God, magnifying His name and thanking Him for who He is in your life! You see, when you begin to praise God, you take your focus off of yourself and what you are going through and you place your focus on Him – and He is greater and more powerful than anything you could possibly go through! Praise gives Him the glory He deserves while giving you a sense of hope and expectation in the midst of the storm. If you are willing to chase down your storm with praise, you will find that eventually, the storm will have no choice but to take a time out!

Here's Hope:
The Sun is Shining Just above the Storm!

As you battle through your fog, always remember that the sun is always shining; however, sometimes you have to rise above the clouds to see it. My first time on an airplane was at the age of 14 when I flew to Kansas City, Missouri to see my grandmother on a gray, overcast day. The scariest thing for me was when the plane was flying into the clouds. The plane was shaking so violently that I thought it was going to crash to the ground or break apart. I was terrified! However, amazingly, as the plane continued to climb higher and higher, we burst through the other side of the clouds and the sun was shining! To this very day, whenever I fly and there are cloudy conditions, I anticipate the plane breaking through the clouds and exposing the sun. It still takes my breath away! Worshipping God through song takes you above the clouds of your storm and puts you in the presence of the "Son"!

According to Genesis 1:16, God made two great lights: the greater light to govern the day (the sun) and the lesser light to govern the night (the moon). The greater light, which is the sun, has been shining since creation, and it is always shining, whether we can see it or not. The sun was *created* to shine.

However, even before the sun was created, there was the Son of God, who has been shining since *before* creation! How do we know this? Because He was present *at* creation! Genesis 1:26 says *"Let Us make mankind in Our image, in Our likeness..."* The use of *"Us"* and *"Our"* in this scripture make this a Trinitarian statement that suggests that God the Father was not alone at creation; God the Son and God the Holy Spirit were also present.

This is confirmed in John 1:1 where it says, *"In the beginning was the Word, and the Word was with God, and the Word was God."* Verse 14 goes on to say, *"And the Word became flesh and dwelt among us..."* The Word is Jesus Christ, God's only Son. He was there before Creation, He is here now, and He will be here after the earth passes away!

The Son is always shining, but you must first break through the clouds of your storm to be able to see Him. Breaking through the clouds will be a turbulent experience, and you might even feel like you are falling apart. However, just keep praising Him until your breakthrough comes! Sing a new song or sing an old song – just be sure to sing a song to the heavens, for if you are diligent to use your praise to rise above the storm clouds, eventually, you *will* see the Son! God inhabits the praises of His people, especially during a storm.

A Flash in the FOG

My routine for years has been once I open my eyes in the morning, before my feet hit the floor, I would whisper a prayer. Immediately after A.J. died however, every morning I would wake up thinking, "It's another day without my beloved son," and I could not pray. After a week or so, I would wake up with that same thought, but then I would pray and ask God to get me through the day. After a while longer, I would wake up with that same thought, but then I would pray and ask God to get me through the day as well as thank Him that I was still alive. By mid-July, I would continue the preceding prayers, but then, I would pray for others.

I decided to take some time off of work during the first week of September. It was Thursday morning, September 6th, around 11 a.m. I was sitting down to do some writing on this project, and I suddenly realized that I had not thought of A.J. yet! In a panic, my mind raced back to when I first woke up that day. I had prayed FIRST! I had thanked God for another day that was not promised, asked Him to bless that day and prayed for others! Wow, I thought, as I *realized that God was slowly but surely changing my focus. If I focused on God, I assured myself, the Son <u>would</u> shine!*

Embracing the Healing Process: Be a Storm Chaser!

The best encouragement that I can give to someone who is left to pick up the pieces after a devastating storm is to take an active part in your healing by becoming a storm chaser! Simply sitting idly by waiting for things to get better by themselves over time will get you nowhere fast. Contrary to popular belief, time does not heal all wounds, but Jesus does.

Whatever storm you are encountering, do not let it ride you into the ground with hopelessness, despair and fear. There are some things that we have to want so badly that we are willing to do *anything* to get them, and deliverance out of the storm is one of those things. You've got to confront your storm head-on and fight for your freedom! Turn the tables on your situation by actively pursuing God's promises. Chase after your storm with God's Word and with worship and praise.

When you become a storm chaser, you will find yourself face-to-face with the only One who can calm the storm. The Son is always shining above the storm. During my storm, Jesus never stopped loving me, and He never stopped being that friend that sticks closer than a brother (or a son). I made a choice to run through the fog, chasing after my storm with all that God had given me in His Word, and He spoke to me in the midst of it and gave me hope. If you chase after your own storm, I am sure that He will do the same for you!

4
A PERFECT FORECAST

Forecasting the Future: What Lies Ahead?

After the storm changes the plans that you once had for your life, what do you do? Before the storm, there were things you had planned to do, places you had planned to go, and people you had planned to do these things with; however, if the storm has impacted any part of these plans, you are now left to regroup and pick up the pieces.

Storms have a way of forcing us to change our priorities, thought patterns and beliefs about what is most important in life. Things that we once thought were of the highest priority now fade to the background of what we now realize are greater priorities. For example, before the storm, you might have thought that the most important things in life were to finally get that big house, luxury car, Rolex watch and a vacation timeshare in order to be able to say, "I made it!" Thus, you invested every waking hour of the day pursuing these things. After the devastation of a storm, however, you are simply happy that those whom you love are safe, together and at peace, no matter where you live or what you drive, and it becomes your priority to keep them this way.

Storms also have a way of increasing our levels of gratitude for the smallest of things. As you recover from the trauma of a storm, you are simply thankful that God has slowly begun to bring peace and hope to your life again. Once you have somewhat adjusted to your "new normal," you begin to wonder what the future will hold. You are ready to get back to life, but what should you expect in the coming days, weeks, months or years? What lies ahead now that your life has changed so completely?

Meteorologists will often give us a five-day forecast so that we can plan out our week according to what the weather conditions will be. Many times, these forecasts are not completely accurate. In fact, they are updated and revised daily, simply because these "expert forecasters" are unable to fully predict what will happen with the weather several days in advance. Because neither man nor machines can foretell the future, the weather forecast is seldom perfect.

The forecast of our lives, on the other hand, is predetermined by an omniscient (all-knowing) Almighty God. Because He knows all things at all times, His forecast for our future will always be perfect! One of the most common scriptures used as a benediction to dismiss church services is Jude 1:24. After all of the evil mentioned in Jude 1 to 23, the writer of Jude says *"Now, to Him who is able to keep you from stumbling and to present you before His glorious presence without fault and with great joy..."* I love this scripture because it reminds me that God is the only One able to take care of me and present me as perfect. God has a perfect forecast for me, and He is well able to bring it to pass. One day, I will be in perfect holiness and perfect joy in His presence. Therefore, in the midst of my storm, after everything that has taken place, *now* I will give praise to Him – the only One who can keep us and present us as perfect to Himself. The forecast of my future is in God's hands. I don't know what it is, but I do know that it is perfect, and I am going to love it!

What's in the Perfect Forecast? | **Perfect Peace!**

A perfect forecast includes perfect peace. In the midst of my storm, I found myself asking, *Really, God? Is this really happening?* The initial shock and disbelief that a situation is actually occurring makes us numb to the calamity around us, while enabling us to function at the same time. It's when the initial shock wears off that high anxiety and pain take up residence. During my storm, peace temporarily became a thing of the past. However, since I know that storms come to pass through and not to stay, I knew that eventually, one day, somehow, peace would return.

As I read the Scriptures in search of answers during the storm, I came across several passages that I have known for years. On July 17th, I read one of these scriptures in particular, Psalm 30:5, which says, *"Weeping may stay for the night, but rejoicing comes in the morning."* I have to be honest. After I read it, I said to myself, *I feel like this scripture is mocking me!*

On July 22, 2012, during Sunday morning church service, we had a guest preacher: Rev. K.O. Johnson. The title of his message was How Long, Lord, How Long? The scripture reference was Psalm 30:5. I was stunned and in complete awe that God had a specific message for me! I wrote a note to Pam Daniels (sitting next to me) that said, "I told God this week that I felt like this scripture was mocking me. Wow!"

When God says that joy will come in the morning, it will come in God's time, not my time. By faith, I believed that morning would come! I left church that day uplifted in my spirit and hopeful that my "morning joy" was indeed on the way!

The question that you are probably asking at this point is, *How long will it be before joy arrives, and how do I know that I am moving in the right direction?* Each person's journey is different, so please don't measure your progress based on how others have weathered their storm. For me, I went back to work after two weeks. It was very difficult, but at least it occupied my mind for eight hours a day. Every day seemed like a year. I went through a period when I thought, *I just want to go live with Jesus.* I was having a drama moment and pity party again.

Looking back, I know that God heard that statement. In late April, I went for my routine mammogram. Within a few days, I received a call back from the doctor because something was not right with the test. Mind you, I had not been called back for anything in 20 years! My initial thoughts were, *Ho hum... I don't care. I miss my son. I can just go live with Jesus.* Looking back, I have to giggle at myself for thinking like this. Such drama! Nevertheless, I went for my follow-up appointment.

A Flash in the FOG

I arrived for my follow-up appointment with the doctor in a nonchalant manner thinking that I would be back at work within the hour. I followed the instructions of the nurse, putting on the little pink top and sitting in the waiting area.

Flashes in the Fog

As I waited, again I thought, Ho hum... I don't care. Forty-five minutes later, others had come and gone, but I was still sitting there. The nurse came in a few minutes later and moved me to another "private" room. She said, "Wait here. The doctor will be with you in a few minutes." Well, at this point, I started to get a little bit fidgety. What if it's something really bad? I thought as my heart began to beat rapidly.

I kept waiting, 15 minutes, 20 minutes and finally 30 minutes later. I started to get teary eyed. Then I prayed, "Lord I am sorry. I really don't want to die. I am just so sad." A few minutes later, the nurse came in saying, "The doctor is ready." I walked into a dark room with three large computer screens, and the doctor was sitting there with his back to me. My knees got weak as I sat down.

The doctor did not say a word, nor did he even turn around for what seemed like forever. Finally, he turned and said, "Everything is okay." He went on to explain that what he saw was just scar tissue. Honestly, I did not hear any of that; I was just thanking God for His mercy! God knew that in my heart, I was just grieving, but He set it up for me to <u>clearly</u> see I was NOT ready to go live with Jesus! I left the doctor's office chuckling to myself. God still has a sense of humor!

I share this *Flash in the Fog* to let you know that as you go through your own storm, don't be concerned if you have a short period of unreasonable thoughts. If they last for too long or seem dangerous, consult a counselor, a doctor or a friend who can help. It's normal for your emotions and thoughts to be all over the map, but keep walking *through* with your hand firmly planted in God's hand, and He will lead you *out* of the storm!

Our Faithful God Forecasts Joy in the Morning!

Almost a year later, I am still glad to be alive, and the tears have gone from an all day, every day occurrence to maybe a sad moment or two each week. Having experienced back-to-back losses (my sister and my son) and being around people who were either negative in talk or attitude, insincere and depressed in spirit only helped to push me into a deeper fog. I would just stay home. However, I believed that it would dishonor my son to shut the world out and lock myself in my room. As a result, I allowed myself to re-enter society, being careful to surround myself with positive people and positive things. Getting back involved in ministry work for the church and being excited about it has taken a full year. In fact, it took me six months before I really even wanted to be social again. Fortunately, after about 10 months, I began to see joy in the distance; it was on its way back!

There was "morning joy" in the perfect forecast that God had for me, although I previously could not see it through the fog. In order to bring this joy that came only after many nights of weeping, God looked past my grief and forgave the over-the-top emotions that spilled out of my heart and through my mouth. In His own time, God finally declared that it was morning, and on this morning came indescribable joy! What did I learn from this? You cannot fast forward the process, it takes time. I am forever thankful that He brought my joy back in His own time – in spite of me!

Take It from a "Fixer":
The World Keeps Spinning without You!

My mother has a nickname for me: "Steam Roller"! When something needed to be fixed, I would simply come in and roll over everyone else's agenda to get it done. Problem solved. Next! I knew how to take control of a situation and make things happen... my way. It didn't take long for me to finally realize that trying to control my raging storm was the root cause of my anxiety and turmoil for quite some time. No matter how much I tried, I could not fix this; I had zero control. I could not go back to the way things were, I could not control my own emotions, I could not control other people, and most of all, I could not change my circumstances. I was completely powerless, so I had to let it go.

One of the by-products of going through trials is the inability to function at a high level. No matter how aggressive, driven, bold, confident, decisive, domineering, demanding and direct of a go-getter you are, when a real storm hits your life, the ability to operate in any of these traits slows down almost completely. Your high-level operations grind to a halt. You're numb. You can barely think or process what those around you are saying. Most of all, you just don't care. It takes everything you have at this point to just keep getting out of bed, walking, breathing and occasionally, eating.

Things that used to be an emergency or highly critical to you just seem so unimportant and trivial in this season. You do not jump at every phone call, e-mail or text message; such communications do not matter, because after all, what could *really* be so important? What could they possibly have to say that you would be even *remotely* interested in right now? Can they fix your situation? *No?* Well, they can wait.

When I went through my storm, I submitted my letter of resignation as designated "fixer." Mind you, this was not a voluntary resignation; I was forced to resign because I simply did not have the energy to fix things anymore. Whereas before I would have jumped at the opportunity to solve every problem that dared to rear its head around me, after my storm, as I walked around in the fog, I found myself saying, "Whatever. I can't do it." Sometimes, I would even follow it up with a "Do whatever you want," for added effect.

It was an eye-opening experience to see how various people responded to my storm. Many times, when a request for me to do something came, it was prefaced with introductions like, "*I know that you are going through a tough time, but I need you to...*" or "*It might be asking a bit much, but could you...*" or "*If I don't get this done, this will happen, so I need you to...*"

I declined them all. And guess what? Amazingly, things got done *without* me. Imagine that! "Whatever" became my survival-mode catchphrase and mindset for a period of time. Eventually, I slowly began to regain my strength with a different focus. I had discovered an important takeaway from this storm: all of the business of fixing situations for others was not my job; it was God's!

A Flash in the FOG

I was having a sleepless night when I opened my Women of Faith devotional on September 15th at 1:45 a.m., and the title was "Whatever, Lord." I almost dropped the book! The scripture was Colossians 1:20, which says "To this end I labor, struggling with all of His energy, which so powerfully works in me." The author, Barbara Johnson, talked about calamity in her life, the death of two sons and how it took the life and energy out of her. She said that just blinking her eyes wore her out (*giggle*)!

This devotional spoke directly to my lack of energy and/or concern about anything around me. God heard my "Whatever" statements and wanted me to now say: "Whatever, Lord! Whatever Your will is today, whatever You want to do, whatever You use to do it, whatever You want me to do, whatever time You choose, whatever place You choose, whatever person You choose... just whatever, Lord.
I surrender again!"

Perfect peace comes from letting go of our will and our perceived control over any situation. Focus on God and

His Word alone, and He will settle you from the inside out. If you give all of your grief, anger, loneliness, financial issues, relationship concerns and despondency to God and remain focused on Him, He will give you something in return: peace! Isaiah 26:3 says, *"You will keep in perfect peace those whose minds are steadfast, because they trust in You."* Peace, be still!

What's in the Perfect Forecast? | **Perfect Plans!**

A perfect forecast includes perfect plans – God's perfect plans for your life. When we make plans for our future, we pencil in everything from education to budgets, marriage, children and other ideas of how life should go. However, no one pencils in life's various storms and tragedies that can completely overturn any plans that we have written down on paper. Only God knows what is to come in the future, and He holds it in His hands.

God says in Jeremiah 29:11 *"'For I know the plans I have for you,' declares the LORD, 'plans to prosper you and not to harm you, plans to give you hope and a future.'"* While you are in the midst of the dark fog, it can seem like you are all alone and that God is far away, disconnected from what you are going through. It may seem like there is no way that if God knew what you were going through that He would allow it to continue to be. It could even seem like whatever is going on in your life must *surely* be contrary to His will. However, understand this: no matter what calamity befalls you, God knows *exactly* where you are and *what* you are going through! Also, remember that before Satan could even launch this attack in your life, he had to get the permission of God first!

The way we do things is *not* the way that God does things; *His thoughts are higher than our thoughts and His ways are higher than our ways* (Isaiah 55:8-9). If you had a choice of how to get yourself to a certain point in life, you would carefully orchestrate a strategic plan to get yourself there according to your intellect. Your plan probably wouldn't include any trauma, pain or devastation! Well, God has somewhere that He is trying to get you to in life, and because He is sovereign, He will get you there however He wants. Sometimes, the process that He uses to get us there is called calamity – a storm. Regardless of the process He uses to get you where you need to be in life, just know that He is never working randomly; He is always working according to a plan – His plan – and this plan is not for your harm or destruction but for your hope and your future. The bottom line: when you're going through calamity, trust that it is all a part of God's perfect plan!

No matter how much we pray, serve, or how much Bible knowledge we possess, things do not always turn out like we planned. In any case, rest assured that the things we go through will enlarge our faith and the faith of those around us. In spite of an unexpected storm, God still knows the plans He has for your life. The scripture says that God will "give" us a hope and a future, so it is our job to receive what He gives to us!

Believe It or Not, the Storm Was a Part of God's Plan for Your Life!

In 2001, I began to keep prayer journals. I had a prayer journal for my husband, my daughter, my son and a general journal for prayer requests. My purpose was to use these journals as a reminder of God's faithfulness in my life. Additionally, I wanted to share the journals with my children once they became young adults to show them how God answers prayer.

I would occasionally read the journals to encourage myself and remind myself of what God had already done. My husband has a habit of writing the date and time on anything that he reads. For whatever reason, I adopted this same practice as my own. I began to date and time stamp anything that I read, being sure to note specific events that I was either praying about or thanking God for on that day. Every one of my devotional books, *Daily Bread* guides, favorite scriptures, quotes, sermons, etc., had been date and time stamped.

Over the years, through this practice, I created memorials commemorating specific times when God had spoken to specific situations in my life at just the right time.

A Flash in the FOG

In 2008, I thought that I was being led to write a book entitled "Broken Furniture." I began writing, but things never seemed to come together. I stopped the project thinking that God did not tell me to do it. People would sometimes mention in passing, "You should write a book!" Being hard-headed like I am, I would just ignore their comments.

Shortly after that, a group of new employees at my job was attending training in a classroom next to my office. I had not been introduced to any of the people in the class. During one of the breaks, a lady walked past my office. She backed up and stepped into my office to introduce herself. She said, "My name is Kenesia Mouton, and I am one of the new hires in today's training class. I wanted to introduce myself to you." I welcomed her to the company, we had some small talk, and she walked away.

Seconds later, she backed up, poked her head into my office, and said, "I have to say this, so please excuse me. God told me to tell you to finish that book." The stunned look on my face must have spoken volumes to her; she simply smiled and walked off. I began to write again. However, I was not consistent, so I got off track.

In 2010, my coworker Nancy McKinnon walked into my office to say her farewells as she headed for retirement. She gave me a beautiful prayer box and some wise counsel, and then, off she went. Seconds later, she popped her head back into my office and said, "You should write a book." I just started to cry.

God knows the plans that He has for us, and He knows *us* – especially those of us who are hard-headed! He gently continues to push us in the direction of His divine plan using friends, strangers and even enemies to drive home His messages. God knew the plans that He had for me to write this book and others. He led me to discipline myself as I wrote in my journals. He also had me to document the ways in which He had answered prayers, and He even inspired me to make them specific with time and date stamps. These little details, for me, further affirm that God is concerned about the details of our lives every minute of every day.

Because of the God-inspired discipline that I was given to write this book, even during my storm, I was on autopilot with my date and time stamping of the things that God had done and said. I did not know why, and to be honest, in my pain, I did not care. However, one thing that I do know is this: God's forecast for me is perfect, and it will come to pass.

In the midst of planning out my new book, my storm hit. Like many of you, when storms occur in my life, the first thing I ask myself is, *What did I do wrong? Am I doing what God wanted me to do? Did God really tell me to write a book?* When I started my book project, my beloved son was aware of my new venture, and he promised to paint my book cover for me. We talked about it on January 10th, and I sent him the title of the book at 9:30 that evening.

Sitting at my desk at home on March 16th, A.J.'s birthday, I was overwhelmed with what would not be. As I talked to God, I remember saying

that I could not finish the book because A.J. was not there to paint the picture for the cover. It was obvious that God did not plan for me to be a writer, because otherwise, A.J. would still have been there. I promise you that I am not crazy... but I heard a still small voice say "Go look at the picture hanging on your bedroom wall." I got up, wiped my tears and went downstairs to my bedroom.

A framed painting that had been hanging on my wall for two years, painted by my son, was the perfect picture for the cover of my book Broken Furniture. It was a painting of an empty chair with my husband's blue shirt draped across it and A.J.'s boots on the floor. That small voice said, "There is your cover. Now go look in your son's room." As I went upstairs into A.J.'s room, lined around the wall and covering the floor were at least 30 paintings and drawings of various types.

That still small voice said, "You have enough covers to last the rest of your life. I STILL know the plans that I have for you." I dried my tears and thanked God for the 23 years, 10 months and 19 days that my son was on loan to me. I thanked God for all of the gifts that A.J. left me (tangible and intangible) to remember him by, and I started writing again.

No matter how mature we think we are, some of us still need confirmation that we are doing what

God told us to do. I am so grateful that God knows each of our personalities, our deficiencies and our hard-headedness. One morning in November, I was reviewing what I had written so far in the little book, and I began to doubt what God had told me to do. I thought, "Does God really want me to write this? No one can be helped by my simple journey through the fog."

Later that evening, after church, I picked up my Women of Faith devotional and read the November 7th writing by Luci Swindoll. The subject was, "Write It Down", and the scripture was Numbers 33:2. It read, "At the Lord's command, Moses recorded the stages in their journey." An excerpt from the devotional read, "Books and journals like this are our thank-you notes to God. They give us a place to 'sing' praises, applaud blessings, and transfer appreciation from our minds and hearts onto a page. The records of gratitude that you keep today will be a consolation to someone else after you've gone on to sing endless praises to God in heaven." The still small voice in my heart said again, "Lil' girl, I know what I am doing. Keep writing."

No matter what you see in your future, and no matter what your plans are, God has a plan for your life – a perfect forecast just for you! Don't worry about the storms: the Savior can calm them. A calamity can't stop Christ <u>or</u> the plans that He has for you! His plan is perfect!

What's in the Perfect Forecast? | A Perfect Place!
A perfect forecast includes a perfect place. What is that place? Heaven! Heaven is *real* – more real to me today than it's ever been. I believed in heaven as a little girl because my grandmother took us to church. At the age of 19, I came into a full understanding of what it meant to be a Christian, and it was at this time that I began to read and understand the Bible for myself, including what it said about heaven. My foundation in God's Word was the source of my strength and hope through many trials, especially when relatives and friends passed away. Because of what the Scriptures said, I knew they were in heaven, and this gave me peace.

Earlier in Chapter 3, I wrote about the dream that God allowed me to have about A.J. One of the things that was most odd to me was the fact that A.J. did not say anything in the dream; he simply smiled. Growing up, A.J. had a gap in his front teeth that we had closed with braces. As he smiled at me in my dream, the gap was back, and his smile was the huge innocent smile that he'd had as a child.

A Flash in the FOG

I attended a Women in Adversity conference in June. In that meeting, a speaker, Jennifer Cox, shared her story about the loss of her daughter, Tiffany. Jennifer and I became kindred spirits and met for lunch on August 4, 2012. Jennifer has remained a great source of encouragement for me because she knew exactly how I felt when I lost my son.

Jennifer recommended that I read a book entitled "90 Minutes In Heaven." In the book, the author vividly describes his car accident and being pronounced dead on a Texas highway. The car he was in was covered with a tarp while the emergency personnel helped others who were still alive. The author went on to describe how he went to heaven and was greeted by familiar "smiling faces" that did not utter a word. He described the feeling of overwhelming euphoria and joy as something he could never forget. When I read the description, that still small voice inside of me said "A.J. is there!" I started smiling.

I know that heaven is real, and I know that my son went to heaven because he believed in Jesus Christ as the Son of God. He had accepted Him as his personal Lord and Savior. Despite knowing this, the God of all comfort is so kind that He graciously confirmed for me what I already knew about my son's eternal destination.

For those of you who are skeptics, let me give you the "inside skinny" that I discovered after the conference. Pamela Daniels was the keynote speaker for the women's conference. She was struggling with the topic of "Women In Adversity" because she felt that the adversities of raising children, caring for husbands, relationships, and other troubles paled in comparison to the death of a child. Pam shared with me afterwards that she had basically told God, "I can't talk about the death of a child as an adversity, because I have not experienced it." In short, she told God "No."

Meanwhile, Jennifer Cox was not scheduled to attend the conference. She opened some mail that came to her church informing the membership about the conference. When she read the mail and saw the church's name, she realized that she had been a regular visitor with the church over the years and considered it to be like a second home to her. She picked up the phone and asked if she could give her testimony on adversity at the conference. In doing so, Jennifer had basically put herself on the conference agenda!

At the conference, prior to Pam Daniels speaking on the general adversity of women, Jennifer Cox spoke directly into my spirit as she talked about the death of her daughter, Tiffany, who had passed almost two years earlier. Jennifer had already walked through the hard places that I was currently walking through, and she confirmed for me that I was not crazy!

During the conference, I did not understand the emotions of my friend Pam as she gave her presentation. Later, I learned that she was overjoyed because God had heard her cry and answered her prayer. She did not have to speak about the death of a child as an adversity; God sent someone else to do it, and we were all blessed beyond measure!

There is a young man at our church named Christopher Brice. Chris is *awesome*! He loves trains and his family. He works as part of the Orientation Ministry, so when new members join our church, Chris gives them a tour of all of the facilities, classrooms, etc. Chris has a very rare talent that you don't see very often: he will ask people for their full birth date (month, day and year), and within seconds, he will tell them on which day of the week they were born! If there was some unusual event that occurred on that date in history, Chris will also tell them *exactly* what happened. It is an *amazing* ability that has managed to befuddle many, and it's fun to watch people's faces each time he performs this talent on newcomers to the church! What's more, Chris *never* forgets anyone's birthday... or their age (*giggle*)! Chris is *awesome!* Want to know another very special thing about Chris Brice? He is autistic!

Seven months after my beloved A.J. died, I took September 3rd through 7th off from work for vacation. I did not have any specific plans; I just wanted to relax, write and clear out some of A.J.'s things. Going through A.J.'s things made me feel sad at times. Each time I began to do it, I found myself exhausted in spirit.

Leaving church on Sunday, September 9th, my daughter and I were walking down the sidewalk to my car. Chris came hurriedly after us calling out, "Sister Poydras! Sister Poydras!" My daughter and I turned around with big smiles and did a group hug with Chris. Chris then said, "Sister Poydras, I miss A.J. He would have been 24 on March 16th." As always, Chris was accurate with his uncanny ability to remember birthdays. With a lump in my throat, I said, "I

miss him too, Chris." To this, Chris replied, "Yeah, that's okay. A.J. is in heaven." Then, he abruptly turned and briskly walked away. Marie and I looked at each other in amazement and smiled the biggest Kool-Aid smiles you ever wanted to see! Calling back after him, Marie yelled out a hearty "Amen, Chris!" as he disappeared into the building.

On October 21st, as I was standing in the church office talking with a couple of visitors, Chris walked up and did his thing: he asked them their birthdates and then immediately told them the days of the week on which they were born. Then, he asked them if they were left-handed or right-handed. One of them said "Left-handed." "A.J. is left-handed," Chris said. Then, he quickly corrected himself and said, "A.J. was left-handed. He is in heaven now, and he writes with both hands." Then, he quickly walked away!

Christopher Brice runs with the angels! I believe that the deep things of God are hidden from most of us, but I believe that God shares special things with Chris. God used Chris to deliver hidden truths, not only to me but to others as well. God used Chris Brice to deliver specific messages to my hurting heart, but He also has a specific message for you in your own storm. Are you expecting Him to speak? Do you want Him to show up? Are you listening for His still small voice?

A Romans Roadmap: How to Get to that "Perfect Place"

God has prepared a perfect place for everyone who believes: heaven! In heaven, storms will cease to exist, and sickness and death will be no more. This perfect forecast was put into motion over 2,000 years ago when God sent His only Son to earth to pay the penalty for our sins.

Again, because of its critical importance, I re-introduce to you this scenario: imagine that you are standing at heaven's gate and God says, *"Give Me one reason why I should let You into heaven."* What would your answer be?

If you cannot answer this question with absolute confidence, it is possible that you are not a part of this perfect forecast. Heaven is not a place for people who have lived perfect lives; it is a place for people who have admitted that they are not perfect. However, they believe in the perfection of Jesus Christ and that He paid the penalty for their sinful imperfections. If you are not absolutely sure that you are going to heaven when you die, there is a way to be absolutely sure.

First: You must understand that God loves you and has a perfect plan for your life. The Bible says in John 3:16 that

"God so loved the world that He gave His one and only Son, that whoever believes in Him shall not perish but have eternal life."

Second: There are no perfect people, only a perfect God. Romans 3:23 says *"All have sinned (any thought, action, or words that are not like God) and fall short of the glory of God."*

Third: There are consequences and penalties for sin. The Bible says in Romans 6:23 that *"The wages of sin is death (spiritual separation from God)."* To avoid the penalty of sin, you can activate God's perfect plan in your life. The Bible says in Romans 10:9 that if you *"Confess with your mouth that Jesus is Lord and believe in your heart that God raised Him from the dead, you will be saved."* "Saved from what?" you might be asking. You will be saved from the penalty of sin and saved from eternal separation from God. This means that you will live eternally in heaven, a perfect place. One of the things that I like about this scripture is that after the word "saved," there is a period, not a comma. There are no other stipulations to being saved. The scripture does not say "saved if you are sinless," "saved if you have a certain income," "saved if you are of a certain race," or "saved if you live in a certain community." It says "saved" – period! That is awesome news!

God has a perfect forecast for you. He knows the plans

that He has for you, plans for an eternal future with Him. It is a perfect plan that was set in place before the foundation of the world. In order to experience God's plan for your life and to recognize Him in action throughout your life, you must be a believer in Jesus Christ. I personally have a perfect forecast of blue skies and plenty of "Son Shine" because I have a relationship with Christ, and you can, too! Hope to see you in heaven!

5
THIS LITTLE LIGHT OF MINE

Waiting for the Strength to Shine

This little light of mine, I'm going to let it shine, let it shine, let it shine, let it shine! Growing up in church over the years, I had probably sung this song hundreds of times. We all know that we have a light to shine for the Lord; however, the brutality of a storm can make your light feel like a candle in the midst of a car wash! Even as I walked through my fog, my light was flickering, and I could not do anything about it. I felt like my very soul was slipping away into the darkness. I did not realize it at the time, but our lights shine their brightest in the dark!

During the foggy months, God had me on auto-pilot; I was just "being" without any effort on my part. When I would try to do something in my own strength, I would return weaker than before. Something as simple as attending a meeting or teaching a class would lead to utter exhaustion from which it would take days to recover. However, life does not stop just because you are in a storm! For this reason, I pressed on, trying to will myself to have the physical energy to get back into the swing of things.

For example, we have an Annual Leader's Workshop at our church. In late July, I started setting classes for the workshop and looking at meeting locations, catering options and even gift bags with the church name and logo. I got as far as an outline, pricing and mock-ups. After that, I was mentally, spiritually and physically exhausted. This taught me an important lesson: I discovered that in ministry, if you are not strengthened from the inside *by* God, you cannot do a thing *for* God! The date for the conference came and passed, the world was still on its axis, and the church was still functioning; thus, I knew that everything would continue to move and progress without me. Still, I was ready to get active again.

Although my mind told me that I could do it, once I tried to get back to my regularly-scheduled activities, I quickly discovered that I did not have it in me. After several attempts to move forward in my own strength and timing, I finally said, *"God if You want me to do anything, You will have to do it, because I don't have the strength. I am just going to wait, and if You don't do it, then it won't get done!"* Before I could complete my thought, the still small voice inside of me reminded me of God's Word in Isaiah 40:31, which says *"Those that wait upon the Lord shall renew their strength, they shall mount up with wings like eagles, they shall run and not grow weary, they shall walk and not faint."*

Waiting for God's clear direction and strength was the key for me. In His wisdom, God knew what the months ahead would hold for our church family. Several people transitioned to heaven, and it seemed like every week, we were having funerals. Fitting in a leadership conference would have been difficult and taxing for me during this season. Thus, rather than diving in and busying myself with other things prematurely, I heeded the instruction of the Lord. God told me to wait on Him, so wait, I did!

Charging Your Little Light:
Prayer, People, & Purpose

It is critical that we listen to God's voice and wait on His timing in three areas in particular so that we can ensure that our light shines as brightly as possible after a storm: Prayer, People and Purpose.

Prayer: It Brightens Your Light!

Prayer is simply talking to God. In the beginning of my storm, I could not talk to Him, and I could not pray. Honestly, I did not *want* to talk and I did not *want* to pray.

Sometimes, things and people become so familiar that we take them for granted. I was oblivious to the fact that right in my home, I was being strengthened by God's Word daily through the *Meet Me @ The Cross! Prayer Ministry*. For well over a year now, along with more than 200 others, I was receiving daily text messages with a scripture and prayer request at the noon hour. The leader of this ministry was my own husband! I loved getting this reminder each day. I would not only read the scripture that was sent but the entire chapter surrounding it, and then I would pray during my lunch hour at work.

Like clockwork, each day around 12:30ish, my husband would call me at work and ask, "How was your MM@TC!?" (Meet Me @ The Cross) In the darkest days of my storm, the scriptures were specifically targeted for me. Being one flesh, Lumus knew when I was particularly down, and the scripture for that day would be right on target.

After I would open my office door following the lunch hour, I was refreshed and encouraged by God's Word and my prayer time. Many of those times were spent in tears, releasing those things that would never be and receiving a supernatural comfort that words cannot explain. All things were being settled "At The Cross," subtly, one day at a time. Strength was being provided, and my little light was being charged for service by God's power!

The *Meet Me @ The Cross! Prayer Ministry,* along with my newly-found scriptures, quickly led me back to a strong prayer time. God knows all about me; He knew me in my mother's womb, He knew my personality, He knew everything I'd ever experience and He knew that I would need to be pushed back into prayer after the storm. Who better to do the pushing than my accountability partner – my husband? Once I accepted the fact that God already knew what I was thinking, I began to say it out loud to Him, and *Oh my, did I say it*! In the divine darkness, I would spill out everything that I had been holding inside for fear of disrespecting the Almighty God. Looking back, I could see God laugh lovingly, but also having empathy, because Jesus wept.

I recall vividly asking God *Why?*, yelling at Him about what He promised in His Word, telling Him how unfair it was, explaining all of the work that I did for the kingdom and expressing that A.J. was my only biological child, my only son (I'm sure God got a giggle out of *that* statement). I would go on and on. After I was finished, I did not receive any answers, but boy did I feel better! After quite a while, there in the darkness, that still small voice would whisper *"Lil' girl, are you done?"*

The scripture says in Romans 8:38-39: *"For I am convinced that neither death nor life, neither angels nor demons, neither the present nor the future, nor any powers, neither height nor depth, nor anything else in all creation, will be able to separate us from the love of God that is in Christ Jesus our Lord."* There is a freedom and a release that we experience in prayer because we know that without a doubt that God loves us, and nothing we say or do can ever stop that love. I experienced this freedom in prayer as I used these times with God to fight my way through the fog! Each time I entered into His presence to pray, my little light was being charged at the cross. The refrain from the old familiar song rings in my ear:

> *At the cross, at the cross*
> *Where I first saw the light*
> *And the burden of my heart rolled away*
> *It was there by faith*
> *I received my sight*
> *And now I am happy all the day!*

Prayer changes the person who prays! Whatever storm you are in, if you will only pray, God will change things and strengthen you for His service. When you are in a storm, your main concern is protection, relief and deliverance; therefore, as you pray, do not be concerned about eloquence, correct sentence structure, or making your appeal in a formal way. I promise you that a sincere cry of "Help me, Jesus" will suffice! He will hear you, and He will answer!

Even when you can't say anything, God understands your thoughts from afar off. Psalm 139:1-2 says *"You have searched me, Lord and You know me. You know when I sit and when I rise; You perceive my thoughts from afar."* Further, when life is so painful that we cannot articulate our requests with words, God understands our groans. Romans 8:26 says *"The Holy Spirit makes intercession and interprets our groans, the things that we can't say."* I know that when all I could do was groan during my prayer time, God answered those unintelligible prayers. They could not be expressed with words, but they were carried as unspoken prayers to God.

Even if all you can do is cry during your prayer time, just cry. The Word of God says in Psalm 126:5 that *"They that sow in tears shall reap in joy."* Whatever your condition, the key is to press your way through to your prayer closet and continue in prayer, even when you don't hear any answers, see anything changing or feel anything happening. God hears each of your prayers, and He is working behind the scenes. One day, out of nowhere, answers will manifest themselves, and you will realize what so many others have: He'd heard you all along!

Through prayer, anything and anyone that is not of God will fall away from your life like boosters off of a rocket, and the peace that surpasses all understanding will settle into your soul. Trust me!

People: **They Are Attracted to the Light!**

People are the "so loved" of God. John 3:16 says that *"God so loved the world that He gave His only begotten Son, that whoever believes in Him shall not perish but have everlasting life."* According to Psalm 34:18, *"God is even closer to us when we are brokenhearted and crushed in spirit."*

As God began to brighten my little light and bring me out of the fog, I was even more aware of other people who were going through some type of storm of their own. Through prayer, I began to understand that the levels of suffering that people experience are as unique as the individuals themselves. I was especially cognizant of people who were suffering due to bereavement. A recurring thought for me was *Lord, I don't want anyone to go through what I have been through, especially those who don't know You like I do.*

Early on during my storm, God began to heighten my awareness of the suffering around me, and I was being driven to encourage and support others who were going through storms. I did not really understand why or how I had the energy to reach out to other people, but God did it. God does not waste our suffering; if we allow Him to, He will use it.

While in the darkness of my fog, I felt absolutely terrorized every Monday! I would wake up in the pre-dawn hours and was unable to go back to sleep. I *hated* Mondays with a passion. I did not know what to do, but I knew I wanted the Monday anxiety to go away. By the time I got to work on Monday mornings, I looked and felt awful. If someone asked me what was wrong, I would just say, "Mondays are *tough!*"

On May 23rd, a co-worker and friend, Jacci Abbett, came strolling into my office with a book. She said that someone had given her the book several years ago, and she was re-gifting it to me. The book was entitled "Every Monday Matters: 52 Ways to Make a Difference" by Matthew Emerzian and Kelly Bozza. It contained a different activity for each of the 52 Mondays of the calendar year.

The very next Monday, I started by turning off the TV (as instructed by the book) and making a list of what mattered most to me. When I got to the 4th Monday, the activity was to send a note to encourage someone. That was it! Immediately, 1 Corinthians 1:3-4 came back to me: "Comfort those with the comfort you have received..."

After that Monday, I began sending cards to people as God placed their names on my heart. I looked forward to doing it each Monday because it was my way of turning something bad into something good. As I encouraged others, I encouraged myself! Now, I look forward to Mondays to see what God will do through my life!

It is critical that you follow the leading of the Holy Spirit in everything that you do, especially during a storm and after the storm in the fog that follows. Remember: God *will* speak out of the storm and in the fog to give you instructions! We must be careful not to move until we receive these instructions from God, something which can be difficult for those of us who are accustomed to constantly moving. When things happen suddenly, you may have heard the expression *"Don't just stand there, do something!"* You can *do something* about a lot of things in life in the natural, but when it comes to fixing yourself, your emotions, your hurts, your disappointments and your situations, this is not your responsibility; it is God's!

Oftentimes, we get ahead of God's plan by just "doing something." In light of this, I have learned to change the phrase to *"Don't just do something, stand there!"* Just stand! Stand on His promises and wait on Him for direction. He will show you what steps to take to pull the pieces of your life back together. The scripture says in Isaiah 58:10 that *"If you give yourself to the hungry and satisfy the desire of the afflicted, then your light will rise in darkness, and your gloom will become like midday."* While you are on your own journey towards healing and restoration, God will show you how to engage His people and what to do for them as a part of your healing process!

When something bad happens, something good *can* come out of it; however, whether or not this occurs is a choice that is up to us. I chose to heed God's instructions and use my experiences to reach out to others as a part of my healing process. After reading *"Every Monday Matters,"* I began a ministry, *Every Person Matters,* to encourage those who are going through difficulties, those who appear lonely, those who are young in the faith, those who have made mistakes, the elderly and people who have touched my life to let them know that they did not go unnoticed. The response has been amazing! By reaching out to others to encourage them, I have been encouraged myself!

When you are in a storm, don't focus on yourself; focus on others. Life continues to go on around you in spite of your situation, and people need your help! One of the most touching outcomes of reaching out to others is watching their joy increase. Some of the comments and responses that I have received from my ministry to others include:

- "I was really going through a bad time when I got your card. Thank you so much."
- "I did not even know that you knew who I was. I felt special."
- "I did not think anyone would miss me at church."

This is a confirmation of the scripture that says *"Give and it will be given to you, good measure, pressed down, shaken together, and running over, will be poured into your lap"* (Luke 6:38). Whatever you are lacking in your life, give it away, and it will come back to you!

Even though I considered myself a strong Christian, my storm shook me to the core. I had the deep resources of God's Word to direct me, but I began to see that it was not about me. I quickly discovered that my focus was all wrong. I needed to turn my focus towards other people instead of myself! As long as I thought about my pain and my sorrow, I only sank deeper into pain and sorrow. However, when I focused on spreading the love and healing power of God to other people, that's when I experienced healing and restoration in my own life! What is your biggest point of pain? Whatever it is, ask God to help you turn it into joy by serving others!

As You Deal with People, You Must Fight for Your Light!

People are attracted to light, and your "little light" matters to God. Why? Because He can use it to help other people in a hurting world! However, keeping your light burning through the midst of a storm is more than a notion! You have to *fight* for your light, and the Word of God is the best weapon to use under circumstances like these. As you fight for your light, remember that your light was designed primarily to shine in this world's darkness and introduce the unsaved to the Lord. Thus, Galatians 6:9 says *"Let us not become weary in doing good, for at the proper time we will reap a harvest if we do not give up."* Then, Matthew 5:16 says *"In the same way, let your light shine before men, that they may see your good deeds and praise your Father in heaven."*

You must fight to keep your light burning for the potential harvest of souls that will result from your life shining brightly – and do not give up, because this harvest is plentiful! Remember both of these scriptures as you fight for your light, as God's Word will remind you about the reasons you need to fight to keep your light shining! As my husband would say, "It's dark out there!"

While some people might be attracted to your little

light, there are others who will be determined to try to put it out. The scripture says in John 3:16 that *"God so loved the world that He gave His only begotten Son, that whoever believes in Him should not perish, but have everlasting life."* However, all of God's "so loved" people are not always so lovable! I would be remiss if I were not honest about the diversity of personalities and responses that you are likely to experience from other people as you go through your storm.

For example, there will be people who naturally conclude that you are in a storm because you must have done something wrong. These types of people may be individuals who do not know the Word of God or who possibly do not know God at all. They closely resemble Job's friends, Eliphaz, Bildad and Zophar (*giggle*). They will try to get you to admit what you have done to deserve the storm, chastise you for not living a life pleasing to God, and find some reason to justify why you are going through what you are going through. It is important that you do not allow this type of talk to settle in your spirit. You see, we can be right in the middle of God's will while being right in the middle of a storm that is a part of God's will. How should you do with these people? Simply learn to pray for them – from afar!

It's natural to expect the people who are closest to you to be the most supportive during your storm; however, do not be disappointed when they are not. God will use complete strangers and even distant associates with whom you only occasionally interact to step into your storm and ride it out with you to the very end. They are the "After the Storm Crowd," people who will help you rebuild and pick up the pieces of your devastated life. In this rebuilding process, God will close some relationships and allow new ones to begin. Most importantly, these new relationships can be related to a new level of ministry in your life. It's truly amazing!

Watch Your Light around "Well-Meaning" People!

As you reach out to other people, your good intentions and deeds may not always be well received; they might even be misconstrued. In Chapter 2, I described how I had read a devotional a year earlier and wrote a prayer asking God to help me remember the story and the scripture to encourage someone else or myself when my turn came. I shared that story with a group of women, and one lady's comment was, "That's why you have to be careful of what you pray for." Needless to say, I was not expecting *that* response!

I was saddened in my spirit to think that a Christian could be cynical enough to believe that if I had been more careful about how I prayed, then my son and my sister would still be alive. Is God not sovereign? Does He not see our hearts? Is He unable to interpret our prayers? Be careful of some of God's "so loved" people that will try to put your light out!

On another occasion, I had not seen a particular lady at church for a few Sundays, so I sent her a card. She came to church the next Sunday and said, "I got your card. You must want something from me." I assured her that I did not want anything, but she was still leery of my motive. Despite the fact that she misinterpreted my intentions, there is an upside to the story: I have seen her at church more regularly!

Well-meaning people will often say the wrong thing to people in a storm out of sheer ignorance. Prayer helped me to understand that they did not know any better and that they meant no harm. I can laugh at them now, but at the time, their words were very painful. They would offer statements like:

- "You will be alright."
- "It's time to move on."
- "Let it go!"
- "When this happened to me, this is what I did...."
  (my personal favorite!)

In addition to people who did not know what to say at all, there were also well-meaning Christians who knew the Bible and would quote it to me at the absolute *worst* times.

People would say things like:

- "Jesus wept."
- "He won't put more on you than you can bear."
- "All things work together for good."

It was only God who kept me from screaming "*Stop!*" each time I heard one of these quotes. Author Barbara Johnson calls these quick quotes "Bible bullets," because they shoot you right in a heart that's already broken. Again, over time, I learned that people meant well. They just did not know what to say, when to say it or how to say it. One well-meaning lady even said to me, "Put your big girl shoes on for this one!" I told her that I threw those shoes away.

How to Be a "Storm Shelter" for Someone in a Storm

Through my own experience, I asked God to keep me from adding to someone else's pain with quick Bible verses, catchy slogans or advice as they went through their storm. I asked God to use me to simply love, listen and gently watch Him mend them. I like to call this attitude being a human "Storm Shelter"! A storm shelter is a safe place where you can hide until the storm passes. You, too, can be a safe place for someone going through a major storm. The things that you say and actions that you take when tragedy strikes your loved ones can either help or hinder them. Prepare yourself to respond in a way that will help them through their storm rather than causing them even more pain.

I learned some very important Do's and Don'ts during my own storm, and God has allowed me to employ them in order to be more effective while I am ministering to others. The following lists of Do's and Don'ts have equipped me to be helpful, considerate and empathetic to anyone who might be going through a tragedy, and they can help you do the same!

Storm Shelter Do's

- Do send cards in the mail. Sometimes, I could not talk without tears, so cards warmed my heart and lifted my spirits. Because it takes time to select the right card, to write a note in it and to mail it, this showed me that the person really cared.

- Do tell them that you are praying for them – and then actually pray for them! If you are not praying, don't tell them that you *are* praying! I know that people prayed for me because I received strength. People who pray can tell that someone is really praying for them. Spirit testifies with spirit.

- Do listen, but don't ask questions. Allow people to share the things that they choose to share.

- Do send short text messages or private Facebook notes if the person uses this technology. These were encouraging for me and often arrived with God's timing stamped all over them.

- Do invite them to an event or gathering. While I was in my storm, my school teacher Laverne Williams just handed us tickets to an event and said, "Be there." We went, and we had an awesome time! Each time I accepted an invitation, the invite reminded me that there was still life out there to be lived, fun out there to be had and caring people who wanted us to be involved.

- Do give hugs, or gently squeeze the person's hand. It may seem simple, but human touch is very powerful and important in healing.

- Do maintain an upbeat and positive disposition around them. It gave me the giggles when I would see people interacting with others, laughing and having a good time.

Then, when they got to me, they would change their facial expression to a "sad face" and solemnly ask, "Oooohh... how are you doing?" I would respond with a big smile and a resounding, "I am well! How are you?" Surprised at my reaction, they would then smile back!

- Do call them on the phone. A short phone call to say that you are thinking about them works wonders.

- Do share funny stories. Laughter is always good, and Proverbs 17:22 says it is good medicine for the soul.

- Do share your story, but only after a period of time has passed. If you have been through a *very* similar situation, share the things that helped you get through it. However, only share the things that helped you if you are asked to do so by the person going through the storm. Here's another important tip: if the situation is not closely related, then *don't* compare your situation to theirs! For example, if you have not experienced the death of a child, please do not say, "I know how you feel." Also, do not say, "I don't know how you feel, *but* when my mother died..." If you have never had cancer, don't say, "I remember when I had pneumonia," or tell them the story about how you broke your leg or had major surgery. To me, these types of responses felt like a dismissal of my pain.

- Do be silent, and do nothing. Sometimes, just sit silently. I remember one Sunday at church, Princess Beverly Butler quietly came and sat beside me and held my hand. She did not say a word, and she did not make a scene or draw unnecessary attention to herself; she just sat there beside me.

Storm Shelter Don'ts

- Don't say, "I know how you feel." Even if you have been through something similar and you feel that your perspective will be helpful, wait for a while before sharing it.

- Don't say, "If you need me, call me," or "I have not heard from you!" I have learned that people who really care will contact you just to say that they are checking on you.

- Don't offer instructional advice with statements or questions like, "You need to...," "Why don't you...?" "If I were you..." or "Shouldn't you...?"

- Don't quote Bible scriptures incessantly or aimlessly to the person, especially ones that are used out of context.

- Don't give advice on why you think the tragedy

happened.

- Don't avoid the person simply because you don't know what to say. If you were around the person before the storm, don't disappear from their life during or after the storm. Although you may have been impacted by their storm in your own personal way, you did not take a direct hit.

- Don't make the person's storm your own or overdramatize how it is impacting you, whether to draw attention to yourself or for other (dysfunctional) reasons.

- Don't call the person pretending to be concerned about them because you need something: "Oh, first of all, how are you?... Great! Now, back to what I was *really* calling for. Can you...?"

- Don't repeat information that you do not know for a fact is accurate, and don't make up information.

- Don't betray a confidence. People in a storm can be emotionally vulnerable, and as a result, they may let their guards and defenses down by sharing things of a sensitive nature with you in confidence. Whatever they share with you, leave it just between the two of you rather than running out to share the latest nugget of information you just learned with others who are familiar with the situation. As for me, I chose to only talk about my feelings and/or my son with people who I know loved him and me.

- Don't wait until you are around a crowd of people to inquire about the person's well-being or to tell the person about something that you plan to do for them, especially when you have never said anything to them about it before privately.

- Don't do anything for the person if you consider it to be an inconvenience, a task or a burden, because they can easily pick up on this.

Each of these Storm Shelter Do's and Don'ts was birthed out of my personal experiences and preferences during my storm. However, different personalities may prefer different approaches. I recommend asking God in prayer about how to approach someone who may be going through a storm, and He will direct your actions. If you operate in love and treat others in a manner that you would want to be treated, then you can't go wrong.

When we are going through a storm, we do need people to offer love, support and encouragement. However, if you are on the receiving end of encouragement and support, remember that the very people who love you the most *might* say the wrong things. The closest, most well-meaning people in your life *might* say the right things at the wrong time. In any case, recognize that they are not intentionally trying hurt your feelings.

If you are on the giving end of encouragement or offering comfort to someone in a storm, simply make sure that you are operating out of complete sincerity and love. Let everything that you do and say be for the glory of God alone.

Regardless of whether you are on the giving or receiving end of comfort, just know this: there are no perfect people, including you. Storms are sensitive times during which people (yes, including you) will make mistakes, so be gentle with one another and give extra grace during this season!

Purpose: It Keeps Your Little Light Focused on Glorifying God!

So, now you're at the point that the category 5 hurricane has already come through your life and left a trail of devastation and terror. By God's grace, you survived the initial impact of the storm. God has shown Himself to be faithful through the fog by showing you flashes of Himself in your dark situation. You have entertained the angels that He sent into your life without even knowing it. Christ has walked with you through each day's journey, strengthening you more and more each day. Joy and peace have begun to re-surface in your life again. You are praying for and serving God's people again. Finally, you are letting go and hoping on. At this point, you might ask yourself, "Now what?" or maybe even, "So what?" What's the purpose of it all?

As I walked out of my own storm, I realized the following about my purpose: it's much bigger than me! It's much bigger than my tragedy. It's much bigger than my well-being. It's much bigger than any person or problem. It's much bigger than *anything*. It's for God's glory!

"Everyone who is called by My name, and whom I have created for My glory, whom I have formed, even whom I have made..." (Isaiah 43:7)

My purpose – the reason that I am here on the earth – is for God's glory. My purpose is to praise God, to worship God, to proclaim His greatness and to accomplish His will. These are the things that bring Him glory. Even our hardships, failures and tragedies can also be used to bring glory to God.

Explaining God's glory is like trying to hug the sun or capture the individuality of a snowflake. So beautiful, yet so unattainable! If I tried to explain it with mere mortal words, I would say that God's glory is the splendor of His beauty, the essence of His power as Creator, and the awesomeness of His perfectness. Since my purpose is to bring Him glory, then I should live my life in a way that puts all of His glory on exhibition, to highlight it in a way that places it on display, draws attention to it, and publicly announces it to everyone that I come into contact with, whether up close and personal or from a distance.

Glory is the beauty of God revealed for all to see. Glorifying God is not something that happens by coincidence or happenstance; it is an intentional act of the will. Even if you don't know or understand how to accomplish something for His glory, just continually say to the Lord continuously "I want *You* to get glory out of this situation." No matter how horrible the storm may be, tell God over and over again, "I want *You* to get glory out of this!" His glory *will* be revealed, and you will be speechless when you experience it – even in a storm!

A Flash in the FOG

A few weeks after A.J.'s funeral, I had dinner with some old friends whom I had not seen for several years. About halfway through dinner, they reluctantly started asking me about the funeral services for A.J. One lady said that she left the funeral service more uplifted than she did when she went to church. Another opened up conversations about my faith, what I believed, and how well she understood the message preached by Pastor Daniels. She did not grow up in church and had never had the Scriptures explained to her that well. Finally, they wanted to know, "How could you guys sit there and not cry?"

I thought, "Thank you, Jesus. The door is opened, and I'm walking right in." I had an opportunity to tell them that I had prayed that people would see Jesus, even in my loss. I explained that God did it. I was not holding back tears and trying not to cry. God revealed His supernatural strength in all three of us: my husband, my daughter and me. He gave us His strength just for that time so that people would see that we have hope beyond the grave. To God be the glory!

Over the next few months, I received more opportunities to share Christ, both on the job and in other settings, simply because of the way God carried us during A.J.'s homegoing celebration. Looking back on the events of that time, I am speechless at what God did. I have to giggle a little bit at this because it was also a reflection of my son's personality. A.J. was a matter-of-fact kind of guy who would say things like, "Stand and deliver!" or "Just do the dang thing, Momma!" God gave us the strength to stand that day and in the days to come.

God's glory was revealed and continues to be revealed in and through my life. I should not be surprised that God is getting glory from my storm. After all, I was *made* for His glory, so anything and everything in my life is designed to point people towards Him. You might be wondering, *How can something good come out of my storm?* I have learned that sometimes, God allows us to experience pain for a specific purpose. God does not waste our sorrows or trials; He uses them so that He can be glorified! When God's glory is revealed through your life, it will make your little light look like the sun at noon, and it will cause your heart to fill with humility and joy! John 1:5 says, *"The light shines in the darkness, and the darkness has not overcome* it."

You might also be asking, *How can I bring God glory in the everyday routines of life?* The answer is simple: run to the darkness and take your little light with you! There are endless opportunities to be a light in this dark world. Many of us can look within our own extended families or church families to find someone in need of experiencing Christ's love. Run to that need and let your little light shine in it. Break your routine! Ask God for some ways to help your fellow man.

Some of the opportunities are:

- Share your faith with others
- Do random acts of kindness for family members or strangers
- Work in ministry at your local church
- Have a garage giveaway
- Volunteer to read to children or the elderly
- Clean someone's house who is ill
- Visit a nursing home and adopt a person whose family does not visit
- Donate blood regularly
- Volunteer in a food pantry
- Visit someone in the hospital
- Volunteer at a hospital

- Do yard work for the elderly
- Cook meals for the elderly that you know
- Give money or food to a homeless person and smile
- Donate clothes to those in need

If, for one reason or another, you are unable to participate in any of these suggested activities, all is not lost, because there is something that you can do that is even more powerful than everything else on the list: you can pray!

When you pray, be intentional and specific. Start a journal or list of the people and things for which you are going to pray. As you watch the news or hear of tragedies, write down the names and details, and then pray for those people and their situations. This should keep you busy for the rest of your life!

The awesome thing about a prayer ministry is that no one can stop it! People can sabotage your plans and criticize your ideas, but they cannot do anything about your prayers! You will find that as you pray for others, your joy will increase and your relationship with God will be closer than ever before. You will bring Him glory with your prayer life!

When all is said and done, you have to take action in order to continue to move your life forward! Knowing that your purpose is to bring glory to God does two things: 1) it changes your outlook, and 2) it shifts your focus to Jesus.

Having anything else as your main focus or purpose for living will certainly leave you disappointed in the end. Knowing God's purpose for my own life gave me an eternal focus that has kept me grounded during life's storms and tragedies. In the grand scheme of things, it's just Jesus! Nothing else really matters!

Finally, My Brother:
Some Closing Words for the Journey

Prayer, serving other people and focusing on my purpose enabled me to "fight for my light." In the midst of the storm that darkened my world, I adopted a "refuse to lose" mentality. My recovery from this storm was not a fast or easy one; it took time, and it required making a hard choice to continue living. While I live here on earth, I refuse to allow A.J.'s death to leave me standing on the sideline in dismay. The human will is resilient, and the Holy Spirit that lives in me will never die. I made a decision to let His Spirit shine through me so that God could be glorified. I recognized the following:

It does not honor my son to die with him or to give up on life. Instead, I choose more life!

Flashes in the Fog, God in the darkness and hope in my storm were the guiding lights that gave me glimpses of God's love and care for me, even in the darkest time of my life. My heart's desire, even in the darkest times, was to have the desire and ability to move forward. However, God knew that my heart, mind and body were unable to move forward without Him.

Looking back, I see clearly the workings of God in the middle of my fog. He strengthened me spiritually, physically and mentally every day, one day at a time. The specific flashes of hope that He provided gently guided me through to the other side of the fog where hope lived. Each unique experience whispered to me, "Keep going. Joy is on the way! Keep walking. The fog will soon lift!" One year later, I am out of the fog and back in the marvelous light! I am SO glad to still be alive!

I don't know who you are, what your storm may be or how long your storm has lasted. Regardless of the details of your storm, always remember Job 38:24-25, in which the Bible says that God disperses lightning, that He scatters the winds over the earth, and most importantly, that *God is in the storm.* If you are in the storm, He is right there with you! I know without a shadow of a doubt that God spoke to me from the eye of my storm and delivered me. If you listen closely for His still small voice, you will hear Him speaking to you, and if you follow His voice closely, He will lead you out!

As I look back over the past year, I am tremendously grateful for where I am today. I would not have chosen the circumstance myself, but since it happened, I am grateful for what God has shown me about Himself and His faithfulness. I encourage you to look for God's mighty hand in all of life's circumstances, even when it's dark. *Look* for Him in every moment. *Listen* to Him in every moment. *Learn* from Him in every moment. Just like He brought me out, God will bring you out too, but remember: some of His best work was done in the darkness!

We don't yet see things clearly. We're squinting in a fog, peering through a mist. But it won't be long before the weather clears and the sun shines bright!
 – 1 Corinthians 13:12 (The Message)

The storm has passed, the fog has cleared,
and my light is shining again.
Amen.

End Notes

1. *The Holy Bible.* Note: All scriptures are New International Version (NIV) unless otherwise stated.
2. *Our Daily Bread Devotional Journal* (2010). Discovery House Publishers.
3. *The Women of Faith Daily Devotional* (2002). Zondervan.
4. *Splashes of Joy in the Cesspools of Life* by Barbara Johnson
5. EMI Music, CMG Publishing, License # 539317, *God Come In*, by Zach Neese
6. Music Services Inc, License # 495722, *The Hurt and The Healer*

ABOUT THE AUTHOR

Arlener Steels-Poydras' mantra is, "Jesus is my everything *and* my enough!" She loves God's people and enjoys speaking at both community and church events and sharing her message of survival through adversity. A graduate of the Southern Bible Institute in Dallas, Texas, Arlener serves as the Director of Christian Education for *Meet Me @ The Cross! Prayer Ministry (MM@TC)* under the leadership of her husband of over 20 years, Rev. L.A. Poydras. Arlener is also the President of the Artis-the-Artist Foundation. This non-profit corporation is a labor of love in memory of their son A.J., and it provides scholarships to students studying the arts.

Made in the USA
Coppell, TX
28 November 2024

41215338R00095